Be Your Own Psychic

by Doris T. Patterson
and
Violet M. Shelley

CONTENTS

Introduction
I WANT A READING FROM A PSYCHIC !   v

Chapter I
PSYCHIC—ME?   1

Chapter II
DEVELOPING MY PSYCHIC ABILITIES   9

Chapter III
HOW CAN I KNOW MY PAST LIVES?   21

Chapter IV
HOW CAN I GET GUIDANCE?   40

Chapter V
CAN I BE A MEDIUM?   50

Chapter VI
WHAT IS MY PURPOSE?   62

Chapter VII
USING PSYCHIC ABILITY   71

Introduction

I WANT A READING FROM A PSYCHIC!

In the last few years the popular press, television and radio have made ESP in all its various forms a respectable subject for discussion, thus lifting from psychic phenomena some of the cloak of cultism and occultism.

People have come to accept the fact that some individuals possess psychic gifts which enable them to see clairvoyantly into the past and the future, or to diagnose ailments from the aura, or to psychometrize an object and describe people and events that have surrounded it, or to demonstrate any one of dozens of other paranormal powers. After such acceptance it is both logical and quite human to want to avail oneself of extraordinary help for extraordinary problems. Sometimes the motive is blatant curiosity, sometimes scientific investigation, sometimes it is a cry for evidence that would make belief in the supernormal possible.

Currently, scientists test telepathy in dream laboratories, hook up polygraphs to evaluate the power of thought on plants, witness a child reading printed matter with her fingers, work on equipment to photograph the human aura, investigate claimed memories of past lives.

Another segment of the population patronizes an infinite variety of psychics, pseudo-psychics and would-be psychics across the world. They go to readers who use tea leaves, crystal balls, cards, the Tarot, palms, auras, bumps on the head, bubbles in water, handwriting, doodles and fingerpainting. There are numerologists, psychometrists, astrologists, phrenologists and telepathists. Their methods and their motives are as various as their abilities and their accuracy.

There is no clearing house for their names and addresses, yet almost everyone seems to be able to find one in his own community. There are no state boards for the professional psychic, no licensing which depends on testing, no guarantee of integrity, no careful documentation of pronouncements, and no assurance of accuracy. In spite of all this, thousands of people permit major decisions of their lives to be guided by help from such sources. Businesses are started, marriages broken, property bought or sold every day on the advice of someone reading cards or palms or whatnot.

This is not to say that some of the advice and predictions and guidance are not accurate and positive. Certainly in some instances such is the case. On the other hand, what often happens is that the reader's hits, or points of accuracy, establish a basis of credibility for inaccurate, and even very negative statements. Open to suggestions, the patron may very possibly unconsciously proceed to make all statements and predictions come true.

There are certainly psychics who, operating with the highest of ideals, have tested, proven and documented ability.* Yet, even these have been known to vary in precision, and certain ones have changed diametrically over the years. Nor can a patron know if his reading is perchance being given on an "off" day, as it were. It would be highly irresponsible to pretend to be able to guarantee accuracy of such little understood ability which is dependent on so many unknown factors.

Scientists in America will continue to study psychic phenomena as scientists in the USSR continue to try to find ways to put the phenomena to use. Psychics and pseudo-psychics will continue to predict, and people will continue to seek them out, just as they have for countless centuries.

The market is there, so evidently the need is there, too, the very human need for guidance, for reassurance, for direction, for understanding. In his lifetime, Edgar Cayce responded to a continuous outcry of need. His legacy, the over 14,000 transcripts of the telepathic-clairvoyant readings, contains many definite statements about psychic ability and many answers to questions heard today, for the plea still comes: "I *must* have a reading! Who can give me a reading?"

And from the Cayce readings comes the answer:
YOU can.

Yes, you really can! Not only that, you are the very best person in the whole world to give a reading for yourself. You are the greatest living authority on this subject, and furthermore—you are psychic.

*See also *The Outer Limits of Edgar Cayce's Power*

Chapter I

PSYCHIC—ME?

Psychic ability is inherent in each of us, according to the Edgar Cayce readings, because psychic ability is a soul quality. The word *psychic* itself comes from the Greek *psyche,* meaning the human soul. Philosophers of the ancient world were often aware of the soul as a force and as the essence of eternal life. Cicero, in *The Dream of Scipio,* pointed out:

> "You are not the person your outward appearance makes manifest; the essential person in everyone is his spirit, not the form that can be pointed to with a finger. Know, therefore, that you are a god, if it is god who flourishes in life, who thinks and feels, who remembers, who foresees, who so rules, governs and moves the body it is in charge of as the highest god governs this cosmos . . . An everlasting spirit impels your frail body.
>
> "Men have been endowed with souls from those everlasting fiery elements which you call the stars and the constellations, the circular spheres animated by divine mind."

When asked "Has the entity any psychic ability or powers and if so, in what way may this be developed and used, primarily for the welfare of others?" Edgar Cayce's reply was:

These are latent in each and every individual, as has been given. The mystic as calls to the entity in and through the Neptune forces, as has been seen as regarding waters and of the universal forces—as is relating to water, as the creative force; for, as is seen, from out of these all force or form, or matter, begins *its* development, and in this relation the entity has his share—and it may *be* developed by application, not just by thinking—but by applying. To think is to act, to some; to others it is only an interesting pastime. *Application* is a different condition.

Q-6. In what way may this be developed and used?
A-6. As given. Application!

256-2

The concept was further stressed in many other readings:

PSYCHIC means of the SPIRIT or SOUL, for cooperation of the Phenomena, or manifestation of the workings of those forces within the individual, or through the individual, from whom such Phenomena, or of such phases of the working of the spirit and soul, to bring the actions of these to the physical plane, Phenomena meaning only the act itself, brought to the attention, or manifested in such a way as to bring the attention of an individual to the work itself.

Psychic in the broader sense meaning spirit, soul, or the imagination of the mind, when attuned to the various phases of either of these two portions of the entity of an individual, or from the entity of others who are passed into the other planes than the physical or material; yet in the broader sense, the Phenomena of Psychic Forces are as material as the forces that become visible to the material or physical plane.

Psychic forces cover many various conditions, depending upon the development of the individual, or how far distant the entity is from the plane of spirit and soul forces.

PSYCHIC means not understood from the physical, or material, or conscious mind.

PSYCHIC means that of the mind presenting the soul and spirit entity as manifested in the individual mind. Then taking the phases of that force, we find all Psychic Phenomena or force, presented through one of the acknowledged five senses of the physical or material body—these being used as the mode of manifesting to individuals. Hence we would have in the truest sense, PSYCHIC, meaning the expression to the material world of the latent, or hidden sense of the soul and spirit forces, whether manifested from behind, or in and through the material plane.   3744-1

Psychic ability was part of the soul from the time of creation, before the development of self-consciousness, preceding, also, the five physical senses.

As to occult or psychic science, as called, then—it is, as we have found through some manifestations, that these forces are first recognized in or by the individual. Hence, as has been seen, in the beginning these were the natural expressions of an entity. As there developed more of the individual association with material conditions, and they partook of same in such a manner as to become wholly or in part a portion *of* same, farther—or more hidden, more unseen—has become occult or psychic manifestations. First there were the occasional harking back. Later by dream. Again we find individuals raised in certain sections for specific purposes. As the cycle has gone about, time and again has there arisen in the earth those that *manifested* these forces in a more magnificent, more beneficent, way and manner.   364-11

2

When questioned about whether an individual could develop such abilities, the Cayce readings said,

This depends upon the qualifications, or as to what is termed supernormal powers. *There is within every soul* the ability to accomplish any influence that has been or may be accomplished in the earth.

If the developing of the psychic abilities is meant here—these might be developed, dependent upon what the entity seeks as its ideal or as his guide. There is ONE way, but there are many paths. [emphasis ours]   3083-1

Again, when asked whether he saw a possibility of a man following a psychic calling, the Cayce source replied:

Yes. Each soul is a portion of the Divine, and that is the psychic or soul force which is a manifestation that cries as it were for expression.

In the material plane there are many manners of a manifestation of the beauty of love, of patience, of hope, of long-suffering, that are the attributes of the psychic forces or soul forces in material plane.   531-7

When asked how to develop psychic abilities, the readings emphasized the need for prayer and meditation.

Q-3. What must she do that she may develop her psychic abilities?

A-3. Psychic is of the soul; the abilities to reason *by* the faculties or by the mind of the soul. And when this is done, enter into the inner self, opening self through the ideals of the meditation that have been presented through these channels, and surrounding self with the consciousness of the Christ that He may guide in that as will be shown thee; either in writing (inspirationally, not hand-guided) or in the intuitive forces that come from the deeper meditation, may there come much that would guide self first. Do not seek first the material things, but rather spiritual guidance, developing self to the attunement to the psychic forces of the spheres as through the experiences in the varied activities in the varied planes of experience, but ever in the light of that promise that has been given to be known among men, "If ye love me, keep my commandments, that I may come and abide with thee and bring to thy remembrance those things that thou has need of that have been *between* me and thee since the foundations of the world!"   513-1

Edgar Cayce affirmed that each individual—in his Inner Self—might accomplish anything psychic. He continually spoke of the power that was in that Inner Self, and of the connection of that Self with the Universal Consciousness.

3

There is within every soul the ability to accomplish any influence that has been or may be accomplished in the earth. If the developing of the psychic abilities is meant here—these might be developed, depending upon what the entity seeks as its ideal or as his guide. 3083-1

Each entity is a part of the universal whole. All knowledge, all understanding . . . of the entity's consciousness . . . is a part of the entity's experience. 2823-1

Today there is a surge of people seeking psychics, looking for those who can hand them the right answers to life's problems.

Sometimes a man or woman who had come to Edgar Cayce for an easy answer to a personal problem received, instead of a solution, the command: "Choose thou!"

Cayce followed his own advice to work for the betterment and the soul development of those who came to him. Instead of fostering their dependence on him or any other psychic, he would give facts when facts were needed, and advice when advice was needed—*except* when it would be usurping the seeker's own decision-making will.

There was available to Cayce's source all the information in the Universal Consciousness—far more than the seeker actually needed. From the records the source selected only those pieces of information which would be constructive:

And from the record we attempt to choose that as may be of the greater help or benefit, and to present it in such a way that it may be a helpful experience for the entity; enabling the entity to better fulfill the purposes for which the entity entered this present sojourn. 2823-1

For us, too, both in seeking information and in revealing what we may have psychically received, the same standards should hold. Is the information helpful? Will it bring us, or someone else, any closer to an ideal? No matter how sensational the information, will it help achieve a life's purpose?

Cayce hoped that his advice and all his work would help others, not in the sense of doting indulgences but encouraging them to *know* their own wonderful *inner divinity:*

Train the mental self to become aware of the divine within, and not belittle self but rather GLORIFY that divinity within self in EVERY way and manner. 2421-2

Recognizing that the divinity is within us is the first step in being able to communicate with the Inner Self. It is also the first step in working for the development of the soul.

Thy body, too, is indeed the temple of the living God. Keep it beautiful. Be mindful of the care of same, and you—too—will think more of it. So will there be more of the abilities to be conscious of His presence meeting with thee in thy temple; forget it not. 3179-1

But just knowing it is there will not move or develop anything. There must be purposeful movement, direction and action.

For each soul-entity enters a material experience not by chance but as a purposefulness—fulfilling that whereunto it has been promised that He hath not willed that any soul should perish, but that each should know and become aware of its relationships to Creative Forces.

Then, as to whether there is the developing or retarding of a soul through any particular sojourn depends upon how the entity applies self—or as to whether or not it is being true to that it sets or chooses as its ideal. 1767-2

"How the entity applies self" is what determines how the soul develops. And if the individual is looking for someone else to make the "right vs. wrong" decisions for him, he is not exercising his will. Turning such decisions over to another person is abdicating the right of soul development—a right that may be painful at times, but still necessary if the soul and will are not to become flabby like unused muscles.

"Decision should be made from self, not from here!" Cayce warned one man who kept trying to turn his choices over to the sleeping prophet. "The conditions are set before thee . . . it may be said that, 'Today is set before thee opportunity. Choose thou! . . . "

And if the man persisted in getting others to make his decisions,

Would thou become an automaton, to be pushed about or handled by *any* force outside of thyself? . . . To act, or be acted upon by such influences, as to be pushed about as an automaton, and to be chosen for us as to what would be the activities, is making the individuals lose their individuality; their personality becomes submerged in that of another. 270-28

Do we wish to reach the Hindu Nirvana, the Yogi's Nirbikalpa Samadhi, or any seemingly far-off state of ecstasy? It is possible only through our own inner divinity; the Christ Consciousness inside us is the Way.

Know that thy body, thy mind, thy soul, is manifestation of God in the earth—as is every other soul; and that thy body is indeed the temple of the living God. All the good, then, all the God, then, that ye may know, is manifested in and through thyself—and not what somebody else thinks, not what somebody else does! . . .

He has purchased with His own will that right for direction. And He has promised, "I will never leave thee—I will not forsake thee," save that THOU—as an individual—cast Him out, or reject Him, for counsel from some other source. 2970-1

Cayce referred these seekers to the advice Moses received from God for the Hebrews, given in Deuteronomy 30, which includes these verses:

> For this commandment which I command thee this day, it is not hidden from thee, neither is it far off.
> It is not in heaven, that thou shouldest say, Who shall go up for us to heaven, and bring it unto us that we may hear it and do it?
> Neither is it beyond the sea, that thou shouldest say, Who shall go over the sea for us, and bring it unto us, that we may hear it and do it?
> But the word is very nigh and unto thee, in thy mouth and in thy heart, that thou mayest do it . . .
> I call heaven and earth to record this day against you, that I have set before you life and death, blessing and cursing; therefore choose life, that thou and thy seed may live.

Speaking of the farthest areas they could conceive of—the limitless sky, the heavens, and the sea, that seem to stretch on and on forever—he tells them not to search far off for the commandment, for knowledge of what is right to do. It is not far off—it is as near as their own hearts! But they should not cover their hearts over with a wall and hide from the decision—they must *choose*. The very action of making a choice for the right is a step in the soul's development!

We must be active choosers—not passive chosen-fors, especially in the psychic field. We may ask for information, certainly. But we must *make our own choices* on what is right or wrong to do!

What, then, is WILL? That which makes for the dividing line between the finite and the infinite, the divine and the wholly human, the carnal and the spiritual. For the *will* may be made one *with* HIM, or for self alone. 262-81

. . . in the consciousness of the entity there is no urge in the astrological, in the vocational, in the hereditary or the environmental which surpasses the will or determination of the entity. 5023-2

It is truly amazing how often we undervalue our own will, and act as if we are unconscious of the divinity within us.

For to subjugate an individual soul to the will of another is to break that which is the greater power, the greater influence in the experience of the soul for its advancement . . . let the *entity* choose! *Do not* force!   830-2

As we begin to feel the intimations of our psychic power, we need to be extremely wary about using it in relation to any other person. Any influence on another that is not a choice of that person could cause harm to the sender *and* receiver.

However, as we express *love* for others, we initiate this response in them.

A 52-year-old woman interested in developing her psychic power was informed that she had lived previously in Salem during the witch trials, when her sensitivities brought only trouble:

Then in the name Dorothy Manley, the entity suffered much for a just cause; misunderstood, misinterpreted. For the voices as heard, the movements as experienced, even as a young girl, were hounded by those who understood not.

Learn ye then that lesson in the present, "Cast not pearls before dogs nor swine." For as the dog returns to his vomit and the hog to his wallow, so will they that listen at pearls of great price yet have no thought, no mind, no purpose for same.   2067-1

In that other experience, the young woman had gotten pneumonia from being "dipped" as a witch, and later died of it. There was no danger of her being "dipped" in this twentieth century, but there were other dangers—including one not mentioned by any spiritualist I've known: that someone in "talking" with their departed husband, uncle, or wife may become dependent on the discarnate for advice and decisions.

Those who wished to become psychic included many of Cayce's close associates. They asked him to give them, through the readings, lessons that would enable them to do this. They expected perhaps breathing exercises, as in yoga, or visualizing techniques. Dr. Harmon Bro, who was close to Cayce at this time and kept in touch with these same people years later, described the group's reaction when they didn't get the expected:

" . . . they were disappointed that he began with the mundane theme of 'cooperation' and kept them working at it for months, until his clairvoyance matched their own subjective assurance that they were ready for a new task.

"Instead of twelve easy lessons in psychic ability they got twelve hard lessons in creative living! They could not get a

7

new lesson from the trance-counseling Cayce until they had put the previous one to work in every facet of their lives—work, play, worship, family affairs, community service. This is why it took them seven years to get twelve lessons.

"But they became psychic!"

These lessons, given through the readings, were later combined into the two volumes of *A Search for God,* the books that are basic to the growth of Study Groups of the A.R.E. Without necessarily expecting to become psychic, others who have worked at applying the principles given in the readings as in *A Search for God* also found themselves experiencing flashes of clairvoyance, sometimes seeing auras, or "knowing" something was going to happen, just as those of Group One did. Dr. Harmon Bro found that members of this first group had become so sensitive and aware that one spotted a vitamin deficiency in one of his children before the doctor did. Others did healing, saw auras, felt warnings, interpreted symbols, and other types of phenomena; not for display or showing off—but for and through their own loving concern for others.

When it comes time for that crucial choice, we can expect the finest spiritual results—but slowly and gradually rather than instantly spectacular:

But as for a preparation, is a sound apple prepared at once or does it *grow* that way? . . . The *consciousness* of the ability to serve is only by service, not by just wishing.   294-185

Constantly Cayce emphasized, "Apply this in thine own life!" Experience—trying it out, living the advice, living the precepts, living the intentions—is the only way to real soul growth.

For "Psychic IS of the soul."

See also:
Venture Inward, Hugh Lynn Cayce
Varieties of ESP in the Edgar Cayce Readings, Doris T. Patterson (formerly *The Unfettered Mind*)

Chapter II

DEVELOPING MY PSYCHIC ABILITIES

Strange coincidences and bizarre occurrences that seem to demonstrate psychic ability are often reported in the press. It is the presence of dramatic quality that makes them newsworthy.

For instance, on December 24, 1958, a Mrs. Lambert was driving home from her job near Morrisville, Pa., when a strange feeling came over her. She had been heading for a grocery store but, following a strong impulse, she changed her direction and went up a road she had never been on before. Suddenly Mrs. Lambert saw ahead of her the Delaware Canal, ice-covered—and about 20 feet from the bank, "two little red hands thrashing the air above a hole in the ice."

She swerved her car to the canal; it broke through the ice in about three feet of water. Jammed ice prevented her from getting out to rescue the child, but her horn blasts and screams brought neighbors who managed to pull out the little two-year-old girl in time.

She had followed a sudden, unexplained impulse, and saved a life which would otherwise have been lost.

There was the story of a Fulton County lady who found a gold ring lying on the floor of the barn; it was the ring her aunt had given her, and it was found at the same hour the aunt, who lived in another state, died. Or the unusual crying of the baby in Forest Hills, North Carolina, that caused his parents to take him out of the crib and into bed with them—just minutes before a car out of control struck their house, smashing the baby's crib to bits. Or the Long Island mother, who had sent her children to the seashore with a neighbor, suddenly seeming to hear her Tommy calling, "Mommy, Mommy!" She "felt" he was being blown out to sea in a little boat, and prayed that he would stay sitting down—it was all she could do. Later, she learned this had actually happened; then a swimmer had spotted him and towed the boy in.

These people were not unusual; they had no history of "second sight"; they were as ordinary as your next-door neighbors. Or you.

9

Perhaps the tendency to equate psychic ability with the dramatic and the bizarre keeps us from realizing the various kinds of psychic ability that we demonstrate daily, and the contribution it makes to our lives. Many successful people—businessmen, salesmen—who would deny either the existence of or interest in psychic ability rely heavily on their intuition, "feelings" and hunches. Yet these are psychic in origin. The readings indicate that intuition should be trusted and relied on.

One individual was told that his intuitive ability would make him an effective counselor.

Its associations depend upon the entity, yet the entity oft questions its abilities to counsel or guide others. If the entity at such periods would rely upon the *intuitive* forces that are as psychic or soul developments of the entity, these may become as the *strength* of the bulwark of faith, even of the house of hope, even to that stay of faith.

Oft have there been periods in the present sojourn when what have been its highest ideals have been much shattered by loss of confidence, rather than faith, in individuals. Yet, keep that which was first given. Know He hath prepared the way that all may know Him. Use, then, that thou hast from period to period, and thus may there come—with the wisdom of the sages, with the intuitive forces of those knowledges of the promises in Him—the greater blessings in *harmonious* manners in the experience in the present.

809-1

Another was told that the troubles and confusion of the last few years were the result of going against her intuition.

As we find from the records, the entity may be said to be "sensitive" to many varying influences. And owing to the choices the entity has experienced a great deal of turmoil through the last few years, for the very fact of intuition—or going as it might be said AGAINST intuition, or to the advice of others without really analyzing the motivative influences in the experience—has brought confusion.

These as we find are as influences; not that these BRING conditions to pass, but they are channels, vibrations that are created about the entity that may have their impression upon the imaginative forces and influence them within the entity for greater or better activity.   1616-1

Intuition is the voice of the divine within, and this excerpt shows the emphasis on the need to listen to it. Listening is a most important part, if not the most neglected aspect, of communication.

Q-24. Please advise the body as to how he may best gain control of himself and utilize his abilities to best advantage.

A-24. Depend more upon the intuitive forces from within and not harken so much to that of outside influences—but learn to listen to that still small voice from within, remembering as the lesson as was given, not in the storm, the lightning, nor in any of the loud noises as are made to attract man, but rather in the still small voice from within does the impelling influence come to life in an individual that gives for that which must be the basis of human endeavor; for without the ability to constantly hold before self the ideal as is attempted to be accomplished, man becomes one as adrift, pulled hither and yon by the various calls and cries of those who would give of this world's pleasure in fame, fortune, or what not. Let these be the outcome of a life spent in listening to the divine from within, and not the purpose of the life.

239-1

Intuition was to be used combined with prayer and meditation; in fact, regular prayer and meditation are absolutely essential for developing intuition.

Q-11. Give detailed directions for developing the intuitive sense.

A-11. Trust more and more upon that which may be from within. Or, this is a very common—but a very definite—manner to develop:

On any question that arises, ask the mental self—get the answer, yes or no Rest on that. Do not act immediately (if you would develop the intuitive influences). Then, in meditation or prayer, when looking within self, ask—is this yes or no? The answer is intuitive development. On the same question, to be sure, see?

282-4

The readings always stressed the necessity for holding the highest spiritual ideals.

Q-2. Suggest how the entity may train self in the present to the study and use of this intuitive sense.

A-2. Train intuition? Then, how would you train electricity—save as to how it may be governed! By keeping in self those thoughts, those activities of the mental mind, those activities of the body, that allow spiritual truths to emanate through. To train such! Not train, but govern! Govern it by knowing that the mind, that the body, that the influences are such that these are not sidetracked from the ideals and purposes that are set before self. So develop. For God, the Giver of all good and perfect gifts, He who metes to every soul that which is the companionship to its activities in a material life, guards, guides and keeps those that in sincerity seek to know *His* way, irrespective of the other influences that may be about a body. Hence, in governing, in guarding, in guiding such forces, such powers that arise or manifest or

11

demonstrate through the activities of the body, keep the body, the mind, the soul, in attune with the spheres of celestial forces, rather than of earthly forces. Rather than listening to that which is poetically given as to the voice that arises from the earth, listen to that which comes as the music of the spheres, that: "Let others scoff, let others laugh, but know in self that He has promised to be *thy* God, *thy* protector, *thy* help, in every time of trouble."

255-12

Imagination

Few people realize that imagination is an aspect of the psychic quality of the mind. The readings often linked it to intuition.

This entity as we find, as in most of the Atlanteans' experiences, requires a great deal of mental and oft physical activity to satisfy, or to fill the self. For it is a very *active* mind!

In giving then the astrological aspects—these become as the innate or the intuitive influences, and naturally there is a great deal of the intuitive forces within the entity's experience.

For anyone with great imagination, of course, is intuitive; though oft may be called by others only imagination—when it is the movement of influences upon the very active forces of the individual entity.

1744-1

In Venus we find the love of home, the seeking of friendships—that to the entity oft appear (as we shall see why) just beyond the reach.

Also we find indicated the interest in things having to do with the beauties of nature; and the *intuitive* feelings—as the entity oft gives expressions to self, and occasionally to others—as to *knowing* things *without* being able to give a material or physical reason for same.

Hence the entity is one having a great deal of imagination or vision; and too oft this has been subjugated by those about the entity. It is *well* that each entity give expression to the hopes and fears latent within the developing mind. Also it is well that this imagination or vision be guided, or that there be given those ideals by which to measure such. For, as is experienced—there is the body-physical, the body-mind or mental, and the body-spiritual. They each have their faculties, their urges for expression; and it is necessary that there be an ideal in the spiritual, in the mental, and in the material. Not that the body should become a hero worshiper, or a mental expert or a spiritual oddity. For, the body, mind and soul are one, and give expression through the body-mental—which is the temple of the living God. Hence those things, conditions, experiences as would emanate as expressions or manifestations of that which is holy, are to be not merely ideas but ideals—to each soul, each entity. And those about the entity are the ones to guide, to counsel—yea, to practice in their daily lives such that this entity may take hold on same; *making* same a part of her own experience!

2443-1

This provides a link to creative ability, another ability rarely recognized as psychic, and in this example there is an interesting mention of the need for a sense of humor.

One who is at all times inclined towards good humor, and might at times well be called a wit. At *times* the entity sees so *well* the humor in *so many* situations as to appear to see the ridiculous rather than that which is the creative force in humor. *Do not* lose this sense of humor; it will oft be a means for saving *many* an unseeming situation.

In the general tend, the entity is very intuitive; and thus creative in its dealings with situations, conditions, emotions, and the like.   2421-2

These innate powers can be misused and dangerous if they are not grounded in an ideal. In this instance we see a distinct relationship of intuitive ability and the person's sincere interest in other people:

Naturally, from experiences in the earth, the entity is a student of, and one interested in, humanity. Thus the entity is tenderhearted; one easily moved by distress in any relationships with others. This, to be sure, may become a stumbling block or a stepping stone, dependent upon the manner in which the entity may use same.

From such also we find great amounts of intuition. The entity *knows* without knowing how or why it knows, and yet all the more reason why the entity should be well-grounded in an ideal; else there may be taken what may oft appear to be the easier way for the moment, forgetting the final development of such activities.

One that may use its psychic forces, then, for either weal or woe; woe if used as a bluff only; weal or betterment if the guiding forces in self are tempered with that promise in the way, the truth, the light, and *only* in spiritual and *not* in *entity's* consciousness or guidance. For, these may become very, very disturbing if there is not the grounding in those forces that make for the closer walk in spiritual things.   1460-2

There must be no selfish motive in the use of these forces.

Q-2. How may this body better develop his powers of vision?
A-2. Through the understanding of self, for the vision or insight is of the soul and spirit force. For, learn that those that are for the uplift or assistance to individuals give and lead to the better force and development. Without the selfish motives must all be carried on, remembering that in the compliance of all law with the laws of cause and effect, with that of the compensation, is ever in accord with self's purposes expended. See?   900-5

Such powers must always be used only for constructive purposes.

We find that the entity should find its spiritual ideal—and not in the mysteries of the East. Not that these haven't their place in the experiences of individuals, but the abilities of this entity in the earthly sojourns have been such that unless there is the whole Creative Force taken into consideration and the entity becoming one with spiritual imports, it may use the powers and forces within to its own undoing.

For the entity takes most every experience by intuition. Easily may the entity, by entering deep meditation, raise the kundaline forces in body to the third eye as to become a seeress; so that it may see the future and the past. But the law of such is that, unless these are used for constructive and never for selfish motives or purposes, they will bring more harm than good.

For there is the expression of creative energies that must be a part of the experience. Don't let the experiences of many turn thee aside, where and when it becomes necessary to raise such; and you will not be able to unless you live that you ask of and seek in others. Let that ye seek be that the law of the Lord God, which is manifested in the Christ, may be manifested through thee.

If the body will do just that, it may become a credit to its own environ and all of those who have the pleasure and privilege of knowing the entity. 5028-1

Naturally, there were many questions about developing psychically. Here Deuteronomy 30 was recommended for study.

Q-1. How can I develop my abilities along psychic lines?

A-1. Study well, first, the 30th chapter of Deuteronomy. Know that psychic abilities of every individual entity lie within self, and that as the body is the temple of the living God, THERE He has promised to meet thee. Do not accept those influences that arise other than from "thy spirit bearing witness with His Spirit."   2757-1

Further details are added here:

Q-6. Are there any exercises you can give me for the development of my faculty of intuition?

A-6. Much might be given, but ye are ready for little of same yet. Find first thy relationship to thy Maker. This ye may find, probably, best in interpreting in thine own experience the 30th of Deuteronomy, the 14th, 15th, 16th and 17th of John; knowing, as ye read same, it is YOU, thyself, [815], being spoken to—by the spirit of truth that is expressed there. Not in the mere words that are said, but in the spirit that moved those entities in giving expression to man's individual soul-relationship to God.

How do you find these? What manner of exercise?

First—seeking! Next—application to know self. Then—in its expression and relationships to others. For as ye do it unto the least of thy passing acquaintance, ye do unto thy Maker.

14

And when ye have studied thus, ye will know the truth, and the truth that shall set you free from those earthly things; not as unto the material bindings but mental and spiritual freedom in Him who is the way, the truth and the light.

Know that this may stand in this relationship to thyself: Body, mind, soul; Father, Son, Holy Spirit. These bear witness as one with the other. For, "My Spirit—saith the Lord—beareth witness with thy spirit, whether ye be the sons of God or not." And to everyone that seeketh, He giveth power to become the son of God! For ye are HIS whom ye worship! What worship ye? Glory, praise, material things, place, OR the willingness to serve others?

815-7

The next excerpt advises living according to the highest spiritual beliefs.

Q-5. Have I any clairvoyant powers which could be developed?

A-5 EVERY entity has clairvoyant, mystic, psychic powers. This entity, owing to its indicated developments, has clairvoyant AND psychic powers. The intuitional, which is both clairvoyant AND psychic, is the higher development; and this may be applied in the teaching—which has been indicated as an experience through which greater expression of self may be given than in most fields. If this is used in the application of metaphysical interpretations, it will be the better for self, and the entity itself may make same more practical in the experience of those she attempts to teach or direct.

But ever know the source of thy information, that it is in the metaphysical or intuitional experience of the souls that may attune to the spiritual or creative force from within—and there IS an advocate with the Father. The promise is in that He gave, "Lo, I am with you—always!"

Q-6. What steps should I take to accomplish this?

A-6. First, it must be lived, desired, practiced within self, in its dealings with its fellow man. Do not teach that which is only theory. LIVE in thy own experience that thou would teach thy neighbor, thy brother.   1500-4

The distinction was always made that one should first strive for spiritual development.

Q-3. Should I pursue psychic development?

A-3. Pursue rather spiritual development; this is of the psychic nature, yes, but find the spirit first—not spiritualism, but spirituality in thy own life.

3460-1

Psychic development should be a natural result, not a goal in itself. This was reiterated as often as the need for meditation and self-purification.

Q-4. I would like to develop psychically. Would it be wise for me to push this development? If so, in what way?

A-4. Rather would we push same through those applications of self to first *understanding* and study of the laws pertaining to the *mental* and *spiritual* phenomena; as manifested in the mental and spiritual experiences of individuals. For these expressions then as psychic forces may be found manifesting themselves through one or the other of the seen forces or influences that make to the material individual an expression of awareness in the individual experience. Whether it takes on the form of an innate consciousness or feeling or vibration or communicative forces that are inspirational in their association and activities in the experience of individuals.

But first, as in those things which we have given in Meditation, study to know what to thy mind is dedicating of self's abilities in every way and manner in which they may express themselves to the spiritual forces.

Study to know the manner in which the body, the mind, may be purified or may be consecrated, that there may be the greater expression. And we will find that these developments will come *naturally* of themselves. In their expression, as we find. 319-2

Q-5. If I have a psychic power, how can I develop it to the most constructive use?

A-5. Each one who has a soul has a psychic power—but remember, brother, there are no short cuts to God! You are there—but self must be eliminated. 5392-1

Dreams

Dreaming is a most important kind of psychic ability, an ability all people have. Dreams are probably the oldest psychic phenomenon in history. The Bible is filled with stories of dreams and their interpretations—dreams of prophecy, warning, precognition.

Dreams come forth from the dreamer's unconscious mind as it is fed by the conscious mind and as it touches the superconscious mind.

The dreams, as we see, come to individuals through the subjugation of the conscious mind, and the subconscious being of the soul—when loosed—is able to communicate with the subconscious minds of those whether in the material or the cosmic plane. 243-5

The readings were giving detailed suggestions for dream study long before such study became popular.

. . . there is not sufficient credence given dreams; for the best development of the human family is to give the greater increase in knowledge of the subconscious, soul or spirit world. This is a DREAM.   3744-3

In addition these readings take dream interpretation away from the private purlieu of psychiatrists and psychologists and insist on the dreamer's responsibility for interpretation.

Dream is but *attuning* an individual mind to those individual storehouses of experience that has been set in motion. Hence at times there may be the perfect connection, at other there may be the static of interference by inability of coordinating the own thought to the experience or actuality or fact set in motion.   262-83

The readings often repeat the fact that dreams and visions are for one's benefit, and should be heeded.

The visions and the dreams, the abilities to hear, see, feel environmental influences or forces—by the least of the elemental influences that record or sound upon the consciousness of the entity—are to be taken seriously. 1581-1

Nor should this quality of mind be one to be feared:

. . . the body should not attempt to consciously prevent the conscious losing itself in sleep or slumber, for through this we will find the first action of the psychic making the physical manifestation to the conscious mind, and with those impressions gained in such conditions use those at once, and the conscious will find the developing of the psychic or latent forces in the present earth plane and may be able to use those manifestations for the development of self and of others. This is the correct way to develop the forces.
Q-2. How will psychic manifest in the physical?
A-2. First through the lapse of consciousness, which the body should not warn or fight against when entering the silence, and through such lapses will the first development show.   137-5

Dream records show that various kinds of psychic ability occur from time to time in dreams—telepathy, precognition, clairvoyance, retrocognition, astral projection. It is absolutely essential to keep a dated dream diary, if one is to become aware of one's psychic potential. Reviewing such a record offers frequent evidence of the operation of the sixth sense. Dream study is the safest and fastest way to recognize the hidden capacities of the mind.
Precognitive and clairvoyant dreams are often difficult, if not impossible, to pinpoint and prove until after the fact. However, they

are usually distinguished by a strong sense of reality and seem to defy any other kind of interpretation.

Hugh Lynn Cayce, who had started keeping a dream diary at the suggestion of his father, reported an interesting example. He had written the details of the dream immediately upon awakening, signed and dated the page and had it witnessed by a member of the household before putting it away.

A dream he recorded was that he had gone with a young lady to the old Masury house in Virginia Beach, a huge stone mansion which was at that time closed up. In his dream, however, he knew that the place had been transformed into a night club. Curiously enough, the face of the person he was escorting was blank—he had no idea who she was.

As they went up the steps he noticed that the place was strangely dark for a night club. A steward came out to meet them on the porch; and he apologized for the situation, saying that a fuse had blown out and the management had to use candles on the tables. The dreamer and his companion seated themselves at a small table; and then a waiter, dressed in a white jacket with brass buttons, came up to take the order. Just afterwards Hugh Lynn turned and saw, coming through the door, his friend Mr. Blumenthal, who built the hospital at Virginia Beach for the Cayce Foundation. That was all there was to the dream.

About a year later he was going to the Masury house, which by this time was actually transformed into a night club. But he had completely forgotten this particular dream among the many hundreds that he had recorded. With him was Miss Sally Taylor (now his wife) but whom he had not met a year before. He found the house strangely dark. The couple were met on the porch by an employee who apologized for the lack of electric light, explaining that a fuse had blown, and the management had to resort to candlelight at the moment. Hugh Lynn and his lady sat down at a small table. At once a waiter came up to take the order. He was wearing a white jacket with brass buttons. At the sight of the waiter, and not till then, the memory of that dream flooded back vividly and Hugh Lynn told Miss Taylor about it. "Now," he concluded, "if I turn around and see Blumenthal coming in through the door I think I'll get up and run. It would be just too spooky!"

At that he turned in his chair and saw his friend Blumenthal entering the door!

As nearly as he could remember, there was absolutely perfect tally between the dream and the little scene he had just enacted. But in order to be sure he checked over all his records until he came upon that one. There it was, signed, dated, and witnessed by a member of the family. That date was more than a year before. It is worth noticing that the face of the lady in the dream was blank, obviously because at the time Hugh Lynn had never seen her.

Mrs. Nagle (a pseudonym), one of the staff members at A.R.E. Headquarters, reports an extremely clear dream which seemed precognitive or at least telepathic at the time she had it. In January of 1966 she had dreamed of a gentleman (we'll call him Dr. Singh) who was to be a featured lecturer at an A.R.E. conference in June. He was, in addition, to be her house guest at that time. In the dream she was talking to him on the telephone and, in the manner of dreams, she could also see him very clearly. He addressed her by name and said, "I'm going to the hospital and I won't be able to give my lectures in June."

She recorded the dream and also discussed it with her husband, but could not get past the feeling that the dream was literal rather than symbolic. Upon hearing several weeks later that Dr. Singh had written to the conference chairman saying that he was going to the hospital for extensive surgery, she also told the chairman about the dream. Dr. Singh had stated in his letter that he had been assured that his convalescence would be completed before the June date, and that he fully expected to fulfill his commitment. Mrs. Nagle could not get over the feeling that her dream had been literal and that he would not be able to come to Virginia Beach.

Letters from Dr. Singh arrived periodically, and none showed any deviation from his original plans. The conference date arrived and Mrs. Nagle drove to the airport still convinced that something would have prevented the speaker's arrival. But there he was, looking older and drawn, but nevertheless, there. That evening after dinner, when the other guests had gone home, Mr. and Mrs. Nagle and their house guests sat on the porch. Dr. Singh said, "I worked on my lectures almost the whole time I was in the hospital and I had my secretary type them up and make copies, but I'm much weaker than I expected to be, and I find that I won't be able to give them. I want you to read them for me."

And so she did! An interesting example of telepathy and precognition in the dream. The dream was literally true. The dreamer, however, assumed some things that were not true—nor were they in the dream. Upon hearing in the dream that the good doctor would not be able to give his lectures, she mistakenly assumed that he would not come. Only after the fact did she realize that she had done some editing and had jumped to a conclusion.

According to the readings, dreams are given for the benefit of the individual, but we must learn to understand them.

As we see, all visions and dreams are given for the benefit of the individual, would they but interpret them correctly, for we find that visions, or dreams, in whatever character they may come, are the reflection, either of physical condition, with apparitions with same, or of the subconscious, with the conditions relating to the physical body and its action, either through mental or through the elements of the spiritual entity, or a projection from the spiritual forces to the subconscious of the individual, and happy may he be that is able to say [he has been] spoken to through the dream or vision. 294-15

In developing psychic ability dream study must be added to the previously listed requirements of setting the highest spiritual ideal, self-observation, study of the Scriptures, regular prayer and meditation.

Anyone who has not already started such a study should read *Dreams, the Language of the Unconscious,* by Hugh Lynn Cayce, and other books on dream study. However, even before reading you can get started on your personal dream study.

First, suggest to yourself as you go to sleep, "I will remember my dreams." Place a notebook and pencil beside the bed. This will help impress the subconscious mind that you mean business.

Be prepared to start writing immediately on awakening. When dreams get too long, brief them. They can be filled in later in the day if you have recorded the salient points.

Break the dream down into separate symbols. List each one and after it write a phrase answering the question, "What does this mean to me?" Now go back to the dream and put your explanation in place of each symbol. The dream will "open up."

Your dreams are in your own symbolic language, which you with practice can learn to understand. Gradually your own dream dictionary will emerge, and it is the only valid one for you.

Your dream diary will over the years reveal the variety and vast potential of your psychic ability.

See also:
God, Dreams and Revelation, The Rev. Morton T. Kelsey (formerly *Dreams: The Dark Speech of the Spirit*)
Psychic Phenomena, Dorothy B. and Robert G. Bradley, M.D.

Chapter III

HOW CAN I KNOW MY PAST LIVES?

Edgar Cayce in his life readings described for individuals past lives which were affecting them in the present. Studying these transcripts enables one to see patterns emerge in a series of incarnations. Talents and personality traits stemmed from them; likes, dislikes and emotional natures resulted from them. According to the readings, detailed accounts of all of our lives are recorded in the storehouses of our own subconscious minds, storehouses we unconsciously tap as we react to urges from some forgotten time. It was the patterns that were important in the molding of the present persona; it was not the places that were important. Yet, fascination with the idea that we have lived before in other countries and other climes prompts us to wonder where and when.

The following questions were developed for an experiment designed to help individuals use their own psychic perception to discover where they had been, their hidden talents, interests, and psychological blocks. It is not a questionnaire to be answered lightly or immediately. It should not be attempted before at least a month of regular meditation, prayer, and dream recording. When it is answered, it should be answered from the feeling level rather than from the intellectual level.

1. Describe any personal physical weakness which has persisted or recurred in your experience.

2. How do you feel about this weakness?

3. Is there one of your five senses which is keener than the others? Name it and give an example.

4. Do you enjoy special sense reactions? Describe.

5. Is there any particular food or way of cooking food which you especially enjoy?

6. Are there any physical types (body) of people to whom you are drawn or repelled? Explain.

7. Do motion pictures dealing with any particular type of physical activity appeal to you? Name one or more such pictures.

8. Is there any type of physical activity you enjoy reading about? Name one or two books involving it.

9. What is your outstanding body skill or dexterity?

10. Note an outstanding physical fight in your experience. Did you win? Did you enjoy it?

11. Have you ever disliked a person? What physical characteristics or traits about this person do you remember?

12. What body habits do you have about which others have complained?

13. What physical characteristics do you look for and admire in others?

14. List the body habits you make a conscious effort to maintain.

15. What particular weakness or physical lack do you complain about most?

16. What body habits do you have which are unlike those of most people you know?

17. Is there any particular physical activity which you find especially exciting and stimulating, i.e., which creates on thought or participation strong emotional enjoyment?

18. What physical ability do you wish for or have you striven to acquire?

19. Is there any particular physical injury or weakness you are afraid of having to face?

20. What physical weakness or handicap do you notice most in others?

21. Describe how you feel about people with handicaps mentioned in question 20.

22. Do you especially enjoy food of any particular country?

23. Do you, when celebrating, seek food of a particular country? Describe by associating food with moods—if possible.

24. Do you enjoy cooking food in the open? Or like food cooked in the open?

25. Have you at any time:
   Liked long fingernails?
   Used a good deal of jewelry?
   Worn your hair in some special fashion? Describe.
   Attributed great sentimental or real value to some physical object?

26. Is there any race or color of people that attracts or repels you? Explain.

27. Do you have a special interest or dislike of any country? Explain.

28. Does this interest express itself in decorations in your home, interest in travel, or books you read, etc.? Describe and explain fully.

29. When you go to a museum, what section do you visit first, and where do you spend the most time?

30. Do you feel drawn or repelled by any class of people (type or group)? What do you like or dislike about them?

31. Do you especially like or dislike any phase of church activity? Describe and explain—first experience, age, reaction, etc.

32. Is there any section of the country which has a strong appeal for you? Explain.

33. Have you ever read an historical novel about a country or group of people which strongly appealed to you? Describe briefly.

34. Do you remember seeing a motion picture about which you felt strongly? What was the subject of the movie?

35. Have you ever had a religious experience? Describe, giving age, nature of experience, etc.

36. What is your most absorbing hobby at present?

37. How much time do you spend on it weekly?

38. How many people do you know personally who have the same hobby?

39. How much time do you spend alone daily? Do you enjoy being alone?

40. Do you make an effort to be alone in the out-of-doors? Do you spend a great deal of time reading, or in libraries?

41. Do you have intense feelings of excitement or enjoyment from any type of mass games or group activities? Explain.

42. Describe a problem which reoccurs frequently in your experience.

43. Is there some favorable condition or event which reoccurs? Describe briefly.

44. What faults do you notice most in others?

45. What weakness do you notice most in others?

46. Is there any type of person you are afraid of?

47. Is there any experience or activity you are afraid of? Explain.

48. What do you fear most?

49. What do you complain about most?

50. What type of music do you like most?

51. How much time per week do you spend listening to this music?

52. Do you remember any outstanding emotional experience in relation to music? What type was it? Describe, giving age, time, place, etc.

53. Describe one of your dreams which has been repeated three or more times.

54. In your opinion, what is your outstanding talent?

55. List hobbies about which you have had strong feelings.

56. Have you ever suddenly been attracted to a person? Describe the person.

57. Describe one or more experiences which in your opinion indicate past lives.

58. After each of the following put down two or three words which best describe your *feelings* toward:

a. Russians
b. Chinese
c. Negroes
d. Catholics
e. DAR's
f. Women
g. Jews
h. Indians
i. Lawyers
j. Animals
k. Snakes
l. Laborers
m. Children
n. White men
o. Men
p. Sailors
q. French people
r. Communists
s. Politicans
t. Germans
u. Policemen

59. Do you enjoy motion pictures about any particular country? Name.

60. Is there any type of circumstance or activity which you deliberately avoid? Describe.

These questions were part of a Searchlight *article in September, 1952. In May of the following year Hugh Lynn Cayce published the following report of the experiment. This also appeared in* The Searchlight.

Four morning sessions of the Sixth Western Conference in Los Angeles, April 22nd through the 25th, 1953 were designed as a group experiment to use these questionnaires. Approximately sixty people took part in this experiment, which was carried on in the following manner:

1. Copies of the questionnaire were distributed, and it was requested that each individual fill out this questionnaire before the following session and return it.
2. It was requested that each individual spend at least thirty minutes each day of the project in prayer and meditation, asking for guidance and understanding of his own talents and abilities, as well as a thorough perception of his own weaknesses and blocks.
3. It was suggested that each participant place by his bedside a pencil and paper, and that the first thing on awakening in the morning he write down any dreams which could be remembered. It was advised that a suggestive thought, "I will remember my dreams," held just before going to sleep might be of considerable assistance in clearer remembrance on the following morning.

This is not presented as scientific evidence but as an outline of a method being developed for experimentation at the individual and group level. Many of these participants believed in the theory of reincarnation and karma and were thus in a receptive frame of mind.

This report on the activities of the four-session meeting of the Western Conference may assist those members who are interested in the method of studying themselves, in further exploring the use of the questionnaire when combined with regular prayer and meditation periods and careful recording and study of dream experiences.

It is important to stress at this point that these three steps should be taken simultaneously, for they have a very definite psychological bearing in connection with the accumulation of data for further personal study.

During the four-day project, each participant was given a number and used this number on his questionnaire and dreams, so that when turned in they could be properly put together.

Case Histories

Number 18. In question 27, "Do you have a special interest or dislike of any country?" the answer is, "Extremely interested in Scotland; Scottish lore; Scottish people." The next question asked "Does this interest express itself in decorations in your home . . . ?" The answer here, "I do not permit myself to indulge in Scottish decorations. To me, that would be corny." A little later we find, in another question, "Do you feel drawn or repelled by any class of people (type or group)?" the answer is, "Scottish people." Later in the questionnaire in answering "Is there any section of the country which has a strong appeal to you?" the participant writes, "I like north central New York because of its beautiful scenery. I am very fond of any part of the country which has beautiful woods, low rolling hills, fertile country. Also like high mountain country with pine forest." Notice that this question refers to America, but the description of the kind of country which the individual appreciates might certainly be applied to parts of Scotland. Later, on another question, "Have you ever read an historical novel about a country or group of people which strongly appealed to you?" the answer was, "Like all Scottish novels; anything written about Scotland, uncannily so."

Next comes the question, "Do you remember seeing a motion picture about which you felt strongly?" The answer, "Wuthering Heights." Further down in the questionnaire we come to, "Do you have any intense feelings of excitement or enjoyment from any type of mass games or group activities?" The answer here, "Would love to go in for square dancing." Then, "What type of music do you like most?" we find reference to "Scottish ballads." Five questions later comes "Have you ever suddenly been attracted to a person? Describe the person." "(1) Scottish young man, handsome, gentle, good singer (2) Irish young man, handsome, gay, joyous."

Thus we find, in some sixty questions, ten specific references to Scotland. It must be pointed out here that one of the questions indicates this individual was predisposed toward Scotland and recognized a deep attraction toward this country. Did this individual have a previous life in Scotland?

Number 51. We find the following answers under "Is there one of your five senses which is keener than the others?" "Feeling. Sensing things by touching." Fruits are especially enjoyed. Tibet is mentioned in connection with reading. The special hair-do liked by the individual is the up-sweep.

When questioned as to the first place she would visit in a museum, Chinese art is mentioned, and the first words of reaction to "Chinese" are "Art; literature."

There are also several references to India in connection with motion pictures which the individual has particularly enjoyed. Was Number 51 in China?

Number 29. Smell is the keenest sense. Spaghetti is the food particularly enjoyed. Number 29 likes long fingernails and wears lots of jewelry.

In describing the section of the country which has the strongest appeal, southern California for the climate, flowers, fruits and sun is spoken of. Later, in the answer to a question on music, opera is mentioned.

Toward the end of the questionnaire, "Have you ever suddenly been attracted to a person?" a person with olive skin, dark and thin is described. In mentioning motion pictures about particularly interesting subjects, Rome is the answer. Throughout the questionnaire one can find several references to violent emotional conflicts. There is an interest expressed in books and pictures dealing with emotional problems. There is a reference to violence in connection with the husband. Men are described as not to be trusted. There is an indication of a fear of poverty and loneliness. In noting her response word to the French, they are described as "greasy." Is it imagination to suggest an Italian experience from this?

The next questionnaire to be considered is not numbered. There are two references to Chinese food, a reference to liking a hard bed and no pillows, and expression of interest in going to Chinatown; names the Chinese people as the people most strongly attractive. The participant likes long fingernails, incense, temples and ritual.

Painting and drawing are described as this individual's outstanding talents and in the word reactions to "Chinese" there is "Ahh! Love them." Another one from China?

To turn for a moment from the Los Angeles project to a questionnaire of one of the members after the publication of the September 1, 1952 article, we find answers to one woman's questionnaire indicating the following points: There is a keen sense of smell especially related to body odors. Question 7, dealing with motion pictures, expressed an interest in nature and a picture "Sequoia." Answering number 8 on physical activity, we have an interest expressed in anything out-of-doors. On question 14, dealing with body habits which one makes an effort to maintain, she lists daily exercise, posture, and some exercise out-of-doors. For question 16,

"What body habits do you have which are unlike those of most people you know?" she expresses an interest in fresh air. In question 17, dealing with the body activity you find especially exciting and stimulating, walking and swimming are mentioned. Under question 27, "Do you have a special interest or dislike of any country?" she mentions special interest in Germany and Scandinavia. In question 56, dealing with people to whom she was suddenly attracted, she names large, strong men. Question 59, another dealing with motion pictures, indicates interest in pictures of Switzerland, Germany and Scandinavia.

This individual had a recurring dream which is described as follows.

May 26, 1952:
   "Somebody carried me down hill, but not up hill, rough going, huge crevices below and above. I must get out and go on. No theory in this but a long persistent struggle."

On July 9, 1952:
   "Strange, natural formations. Sight-seeing. Growing quite dark, though it was only about 3 p.m. I thought 'so I will wait and have just one meal, later.' Way became involved in confusing, huge boulders which I recall dreaming before. I must go on that way. I recall precisely how it all looked where I had entered. Know I can find a way out."

August 30, 1952:
   "High place overlooking water and ocean, many steps and difficult passages, but I got through."

Whatever the origin, this individual is surely involved with many different kinds of memories of mountain country. Is this a past experience pressing through?

Let us turn now to another questionnaire from the Los Angeles project. Here we find in question 3 the sense of smell indicated as keenest. In number 6, in answer to the question concerning body types of people to whom she is drawn or repelled, she indicates she likes clean-looking, slender, healthy people . . . bodies under control." For question 7, concerning motion pictures dealing with physical activity, she names pictures regarding hikes, wanderings through forests and mountain. And also indicates an interest in waltz themes, such as one from "The Great Waltz," which she mentions several times.

In question 9, an interest in swimming, tennis and hiking are given for the outstanding body skill or dexterity. Dancing is also mentioned.

In question 12, regarding your body habits of which others complain, she stresses fastidious cleanliness and connects it with camping trips and hikes. "The rest of the party would fall into sleeping bags, while I was miserable until I had a chance to go down and take a bath."

To question 13, what physical characteristics you admire in others, she had answered, "Clean, healthy, good at sports. Good control of their bodies."

Question 14, in the list of body habits which she makes a conscious effort to maintain, she mentions cleanliness, agility and poise. In question 16, "What body habits do you have which are unlike those of most people . . . ?" she mentions again the fastidiousness about being clean.

Question 18, "What physical ability do you wish for or have you striven to acquire?" she answers by "control of the body, swimming, tennis and dancing." In question 22, on especially enjoyed food of any particular country, she mentions German at once. In question 24, "Do you enjoy cooking food in the open? Or like food cooked in the open?" she answers, "Love camp-fires, and everything that goes with them."

In question 27, on special attraction or dislike of any country, a strong and special interest is indicated in Switzerland, Austria and Germany. She goes into some explanation of the interest in German art, languages and literature, especially mentioning, "I am crazy about Strauss waltzes."

Question 28, "Does this interest express itself in decorations in your home, interest in travel, or books, etc . . . ?" she says, "In art I prefer European, classic or romantic or any other style. I love to travel in Germany, Austria and Switzerland." In question 30, "Do you feel drawn or repelled by any class of people (type or group)?" she says, "Prefer the upper classes. With their position comes wealth and opportunity, thus education, time to cultivate good taste. Less liking for the lower classes. I like musicians, artists and educated people."

In question 32, "Is there any section of the country which has a strong appeal for you?" she says, "Southern California, but I prefer greener country with more forests and lakes. There must be mountains and the seashore." Again in 34, there is a reference to "The Great Waltz" as a picture toward which she felt strongly drawn. In question 35, asking about a religious experience, there is a good description of a religious experience resulting from hearing a performance of Bach's "St. John's Passion."

Question 56, dealing with being strongly attracted to a person, brings from her "A man, 25 years old, tall, slender, healthy looking. He had come from Switzerland just a week ago, and I loved his accent when he spoke English. I liked it still more when he spoke German." In question 59, in answer to "Do you enjoy motion pictures about any particular country?" she refers to pictures about Switzerland, Vienna and Germany which she enjoys especially. And in the list of word responses, after French people she has "Sensual, not quite sincere, fun and loving," while after German there appear the words "Cultured and sincere."

Is it stretching a point to suggest an incarnation in Germany in a well-to-do family?

One aspect of this experiment may be considered only briefly. During the four days, a number of personal problems were cleared up in the light of karmic patterns. No one was encouraged to "air" such experiences.

Now let us turn for a few moments to the premise suggested by the Edgar Cayce readings and try to view the data collected from these questionnaires in the light of these suggestions.

1. The Edgar Cayce readings point out that past incarnations in the earth plane play an important part in the total emotional life of an individual.

2. Karma is a very definite law, according to these readings. An individual, at any point, is the sum total of all experiences in every plane of consciousness. This is not a new idea at all, for psychology has more and more brought to the realization of the average person that he is a complete whole from this one life experience. The subconscious mind records minute detail far beyond physical consciousness.

The readings, at this point, simply extend the range of perception and experience to include other lives in the earth plane, and insist that the mind retains these impressions much as the body retains the impression of food which is completely assimilated and turned into nerves, bones, tissues, blood, etc. The actual food itself cannot be seen, but in its new form it is a total result of all which has been taken into the body as food, air, etc.

3. The readings seem to indicate that each individual retains the memory of these experiences at the cell level, especially in the endocrine centers of the body, which control and are related to all psychic experiences.

The purpose, then, of our individual and group therapy and questionnaires is to explore the possibility of reawakening, quickening the higher memory to bring forward talents, abilities, and urges which would enrich the range and quality of experience. This might also provide an opportunity for conscious meeting of the blocks and inhibitions which press forward as urges, desires and negative emotions tending to inhibit the mental and spiritual progress of the individual, group or race.

It should be made absolutely clear here again that this is not a matter at this point of advancing pat theories or ideas which it is suggested that you as individuals accept immediately, but simply that we *are* pointing out the need for further exploration and testing of these points of view expressed in the readings.

Careful point should also be made here of the fact that it is not a matter solely of recall of details through the stimulation of a questionnaire based on emotional reaction, but also the parallel guidance which may come if there is a consistent seeking, through dreams. There is much in the readings to indicate that dreams themselves, at times, become a type of therapy. Questionnaires, meditation and dreams may combine to bring not only consciousness at the memory level but consciousness at the ability level, the action level, the sensitivity level. For example, if an individual passes through a particularly high period of development, let us say in an incarnation in Germany or Switzerland as might be indicated by the questionnaire considered last, then the awakening of this experience through stirring at the deep emotional level might well result in improvement in the balance of talents and abilities; might well result in an increase in the sensitivity of the individual as he pursues a particular talent; might result in better relations, for example, in a family where there have been past conflicts, but where there is a desire to meet and face up to weaknesses.

It seems quite possible that we may be able to sharpen the questionnaires to focus directly on the pattern which is outlined. One of the most important phases of this study might come through the stimulation of dream patterns which would reveal the talents and abilities, as well as weaknesses. Human relation problems could be helpfully worked out at the higher mental level by the dream therapy.

Not to be considered lightly, of course, is the important factor of the influence of regular meditation and prayer periods which have been suggested to accompany the daily recording of the dreams and the work on the questionnaire.

Each questionnaire might be followed up to advantage by reading and study in the areas indicated by the dream patterns. This might help reveal or stimulate the memory in such a way as to enable the individual to bring through the most helpful aspects of each experience.

If past life experiences at a personal level are a fact, this may lead gradually into what Gina Cerminara has called very expressively "a new dimension in psychology." From our point of view, it certainly deserves careful and thorough study and experimentation, and such study and experimentation can only be carried on by individuals who are willing to take the time and make the effort to explore these inner, deeper recesses of their minds and souls. Whether this be simply a matter of childhood memories which are awakened and stimulated, or actually the knocking at the door to the memory of other experiences, it may result for the individual in greater clarification of the everyday problems, and open the door to a new world of experience on both the mental and the emotional level.

Retrocognition in Dreams

Although answering the questionnaire may not provide all of the details you want, it certainly can supply valuable clues. Details are often forthcoming in dreams when records are kept over a long period of time. Both are valid standards for evaluating any information given about past lives.

Dreams which demonstrate the faculty of retrocognition, that is, looking back at scenes from past lives, are most often spontaneous in nature. This characteristic they share with psychic ability as previously described by the readings—they should be the natural result of growth rather than a goal to be striven for. Very often they occur when a person has been working very diligently on a problem or situation and has exhausted all means at his disposal, and needs the missing pieces to the puzzle. Flashes of a past life are then sometimes forthcoming by way of explanation of relationships to assist the individual in his understanding and development.

The clues that identify a past life dream are varied and such identification usually depends largely on the dreamer's own understanding of himself and his dreams. The feature most commonly recognizable is the setting of the dream in another time, another place, in which the dreamer himself appears as another personality. In other words, they are often costume or period pieces. Shane Miller, in *Dreams, the Language of the Unconscious,* describes some of his past life dreams in detail. He goes on to point out that they were not literal flashbacks of incidents widely separated in time and space, but given symbolically, and answering a need in his personal life at the time. They are, therefore, sometimes indirect.

In addition to arising to supply understanding, past life dream recalls are sometimes triggered by situations which have intense emotional impact: hearing certain music from the past, meeting someone who bears a strong resemblance to someone previously known, finding oneself in a particular locale, or in a foreign country for the first time. Whatever the spark for the soul memory, the dreamer can identify his own personality, and most often see that personality in relationship to other people.

Self-observation must be meticulous in interpreting one's dreams, remembering that frequently characters in our dreams represent only facets of our own personalities. The presence of a famous personage in a dream with a historical setting is in no way assurance that the dreamer was that entity, although too often this kind of star-casting takes place. The greatest majority of people who had readings from Cayce were not at all famous in their past lives. Furthermore, the readings often indicated that past fame was not commensurate with greatest greatness of soul. In dreams, well-known figures from the past sometimes are simply a means of time or period identification.

The following are examples of past life dreams reported by some A.R.E. members.

C's dream:
A lady, dressed in a long, gingham dress and wearing an old-fashioned dust cap on her head, is packing her belongings. She is the wife of General Knockburn. The dreamer feels a great deal of urgency and tries to hurry along the woman, who is slow in preparing to leave. There is firing and fighting in the streets. The presence of Redcoats seems to place the dream during the Revolutionary War.

The woman stands in the bedroom and notices that the right side of the mattress is raised a little, as if someone is hiding there. The dreamer (now identified as a young boy) tries to warn the woman, then races down the winding stairs. The bedroom is on the 5th floor, and the main floor is below the 1st floor (as floors are numbered in Europe). The woman screams. The young boy, dressed in knickerbockers, runs from the house, dashes down the street to evade the Redcoats, opens the door to an outside cellar, and climbs in to hide.

The dreamer felt as if she were the little boy in the dream and that she was reliving the experience. At this writing she is still working with what the memory might mean to her.

E's dream:
E. is dressed in a black Bedouin dress with a veil pulled across her face. She is sitting on the sand and opposite her is her present real-life

sister Eva. She looks at Eva and says, "Eva, I didn't know you were a Bedouin, too." Eva just smiles and nods knowingly.

The dreamer felt this vignette pointed up her past life association with her sister as explaining their present closeness and bonds of interest.

A's dream:

"Never had one of my dreams been as clear as this one, with my sense of touch, hearing and smell all operating keenly. Usually a dream opens with a scene, but the first astonishing thing I was aware of in this dream was that I was actually in the body of a stout girl, very blond and large boned and dressed in a heavy white cotton dress with a worker's apron around the waist. I actually felt this was my body—and there were a few moments of amazement at being in a stout body, since in my present form I have always been very thin. I had the feeling of Germany or that part of the world although I have never been there nor read much about that country. The scene around me became noticeable as an old shoe shop of some kind. I smelled leather very strongly and was handling heavy-looking shoes. There was an old man toward the back of the shop with a cap on and I knew he owned the shop. Then, the door of the shop made a noise and I turned from the shelf I was standing near and went to get the shoes from another part of the store for the man who had come in. There was no conversation; I seemed to recognize him and go right to the shoes. That's the end of my recall of this dream. When I awakened I had the feeling that I had led that life before."

K's dream:

"I dreamt that I drove into a service station, and a black attendent approached. He asked me if I remembered the number 'hung' from a life in Oklahoma. Upon awakening I felt that this indicated that I had lived as an Indian in Oklahoma. The number 'hung' was pronounced much like an Indian word. Further interpretation identified the black service station attendant as being representative of the subconscious providing a service."

The importance of these glimpses into the past can be determined only by the individual as he examines his own associations and interests. Dreams brought to Edgar Cayce for interpretation illustrate the fact that such dreams are often indirect and interwoven with much personal symbolism.

Q-2. Explain the significance of the childhood dream of eyes and bubbles, and how its influence can be used for good in the future.

A-2. These as we find are, as it were, the ends—or portions—of many individual experiences of the entity through many of its sojourns. As the entity knew of and saw manifestations of the power of the unseen forces in the experiences of others, it brought those activities and movements of every form. Thus these become as fearful experiences, or as things that create fear. Yet, if they are taken as assurances of His promises, it will be seen that they are reminders that out of self visions come, out of self thoughts arise, out of self activities may begin; and these become rather then as stepping stones than stumbling stones—as they oft have.

Then, the little assurances that arise, bless them, keep them; not as fearful things, but as those things upon which HOPE and faith and patience and love may be builded!   2205-3

As to the appearances in the earth—these find expression more in what is called the senses, or the physical dreams. For, the entity does dream, oft. It should record more often the experiences. These kept or paralleled or drawn upon for the basis of expressions as may be given in the abilities as the writer, may be of great value to the entity in a material, in a mental and spiritual way.

Before this the entity was in the land just north of the entity's present nativity, during the breaking up of the settlements in the land.

The entity was among those groups that left Fort Dearborn, settling in and around what is now a portion of Richmond, Indiana.

Then in the name Cassie Eversole, the entity was active in home building; being an instructor or teacher in the groups organized in that vicinity during the period. There the entity gained, and yet its dreams of places and conditions may at present form the background of those talents or abilities for the entity to give expression to same.   3135-1

In giving those influences which have been and are as urges latent and manifested in this experience, we find that the sojourns in the environs about the earth are as latent in the dreams, the visions, the real inner self; and thus have their part in the entity making its choices as to its activity, its relationships to others.   2331-1

In the material sojourns we will find influences to the real emotions of the entity—as we find in the astrological sojourns (as termed by many) urges arising from the latent forces, those that are just glimpsed within the mental self, or becoming dreams as it were of the entity.

And this entity will have, as it has had, some very imposing dreams. For as an Atlantean, manifesting those spiritual laws and spiritual truths in material application, these become at times very close to the surface in the experience of the entity.   1968-1

Hence we will find the land of the Persian Gulf, as well as the northernmost coast of Africa, through the upper portions of the Nile, are parts of the lands and conditions and areas that bring an especial interest oft in the entity's experience.

36

And when there are the visions or dreams in the entity's experience (which there have been once or twice, especially), in which these lands enter—that were a part of the indwelling of the entity itself—it may be said that these are from those periods which brought greater aid and help to the individual lands.   2147-1

Q-2. Please interpret the dream I had Friday night, April 20th, in which I contacted [487].
A-2. In the associations there has been that which has brought about much that may be found by delving—as it were—into those abilities of self to harken back to those experiences as in Egypt, and in those that the self brought with self from the Atlantean land—where there were the close associations with these two entities. And as these are delved into, *much* may be gained that will be helpful to each in comprehending that visioned by self, as to how their relations and their associations might aid one another.

The vision, then, was rather an experience where *practical* application may be made by self entering into the inner self, seeing and knowing those experiences to be continued—as it were—in the *helpfulness* that may be given.   540-1

Déjà Vu

The *déjà vu* experience is one that happens while the individual is awake; it means literally "already seen." The person has the feeling, and, at times, a complete conscious memory, of having been somewhere he has never been in this life. He is often able to offer descriptive details which he has no means of knowing with the five senses. Not all of these experiences are valid memories of past lives; they are sometimes memories of a place or situation which has been previously previewed in a dream.

According to the readings we preview at the subconscious level all of the major events in our lives before they happen.

Dr. Ian Stevenson published his investigations of such experiences in the booklet *The Evidence for Survival from Claimed Memories of Former Incarnations.*

In some of Cayce's readings, the individual was told that the area in which he had spent a previous life would be particularly interesting to him, and that he would be aware of having been there before.

Before this, there were those settlings in the land of the present nativity near to what is now Toledo, Ohio.

The entity then, finds many of the environs of this place of interest, being almost conscious of having been in the environs under different circumstances. These appear at times in dreams and in the visions of the entity.

Harken to thy dreams and visions, for these may oft be channels through which ye may be known, be made known to impending disturbances, or the choice to be made for the better universality in the activities.   5264-1

One woman was told that she could develop conscious recall if she worked on it.

Q-6. Was my work completed in my life in India or will that cycle return to be completed, and will I play a part?

A-6. The opportunity is before you! for, as has been seen, the entity may make for itself here quite an interesting demonstration, which to *itself* will bespeak that as has been given as concerning abilities of the entity in *using* the various forces. Be *warned*—do not use to self's undoing! but that thou mayest know, this thou mayest do! Gaze into a crystal, in thine own conscious moments—thou may see many of the spheres through which *you, thyself*, have passed. Possibly not the first, but before the *fifth* time they will begin to appear; for these are a portion of those same forces studied, *used*—not abused—in India, as *well* as in Egypt.

Q-7. Give a brief sketch of my Egyptian life.

A-7. Even as a sketch this may be *long,* but if the entity will—as given—vision in self's own quieter moments, and look upon those monuments as were builded in that period for the dispensing of the various forms of the knowledge obtained and made manifest in the lives of individuals—in most too much a ritualistic manner, which eventually brought to many "Must I give this people water?" *that* attitude, that condition—but if the entity will vision these from the aspect of the uses made of the sacred fires, of the sacred musics, of the sacred dances—as the entity gained the understanding of that rhythm, and the various forms of air, water, fire, brought *into* the experience of the mental man—and as he used same in the dispensing of this knowledge in the various spheres to which he was sent, or went, or *chose* to gain counsel from those combining forces of that as was obtained by self in the experience, and chose to match with, or mate with the various forms of the finding of self-expression in the other fields—then the entity may gain something of the sojourn in this land. For, coming in as the entity did—and taking up the various studies as they began in the rehabiting of those places beset by the turmoil and strife that arose from dissensions in the land—and as the entity gained from this poor, decrepit outcast [Ra Ta] who returned to give counsel again to those who were falling by the way; though fallen himself in *physical* conditions, yet the mind active—and the entity caught a vision, then, and sought to send same forth. *Do* the same in the present.   311-2

Conscious recall often happens in very rapid flashbacks. In these, the individual feels momentarily as if he is another personality in another time. One person questioned the validity of such flashes.

Q-6. I have had flashes of past lives—a Norseman, a Spaniard about the time of Ponce de Leon—one of being on Columbus' ship—a Roman solider—an American Indian. Are these impressions from past incarnations? Please explain.

A-6. As just indicated, the body is Body, Mind, Soul. HEED these impressions. These are flashes at times of material experiences that have been an influence—just as has been indicated as to how ye may develop to apply thy mind in thy studies, or in any endeavor that ye undertake—these become a part of the real self. These are, in instances, material experiences as sojourns. For as has been indicated, not all of the dwellings in the earth have been given. For, as the illustrations: Ye experienced much of the Indian experience through the Salem sojourn—that is, by associations. The Ponce de Leon and the Spanish—these ye will find, as ye interpret deeper, are one. And the flashes as from the Norseman—a real experience.   **1582-2**

Regular meditation was suggested in order to awaken memories of past experiences that would be helpful.

In meditation the entity will gain much; not so much as what is ordinarily termed psychic, but rather of the awakening of self's own *experiences* through the many periods in the earth, and the lessons lost or gained there. These, applied in the present experience, especially with that builded in love, will bring the glory of the life well lived, and the blessings from those who contact or know the entity best.   **417-1**

See also:
Many Mansions, Gina Cerminara, Ph.D.
The World Within, Gina Cerminara, Ph.D.
Twenty Cases Suggestive of Reincarnation, Ian Stevenson, Ph.D.

Chapter IV

HOW CAN I GET GUIDANCE?

The questions put to thousands of psychics daily are often poignant, personal, and cover the spectrum of human relationships. They are posed with sincerity and the conviction that some other person aided by a crystal ball, a deck of cards, or a swinging pendulum can offer advice and see solutions.

What can I do about—my husband? my wife? my children? What should I do about my job? moving? buying land? renting? Why did this happen to me? How can I help——? Who will help me?

The Edgar Cayce readings insist that *all* assistance is available by turning within. No one knows any more about you and your problems than you do, for stored in the subconscious mind, the mind of the soul, is the record of all you have done, thought, and felt in this life and in all other lives. Why trust a stranger, or even the next-door neighbor, when the only trustworthy guidance is easily and freely available from the Greatest Living Authority on the subject—YOU!

When people asked Cayce how to get guidance, they were told to turn within, to listen to the still small voice.

Q-1. How can I use my energy to get the most out of life?
A-1. In understanding or listening to those voices that speak from within and about self. Not material; but those *unseen* sources are *opening* to the abilities. Apply; do not abuse. Rather harken to that still small voice; for know that while the storms may—in all their picturesque beauty—bring fears or joy in the hearts of many, and that the ravages of war and the boldness as created by the spirit of patriotic influences are aroused, these are *outward* signs—and that which *builds* is the still small voice from within. Seek not "Who shall ascend into the heavens to bring him down, or go to the ends of the earth that ye may know!" Rather that that is within thine own self only needs the line upon line, the line upon line, to bring the understanding that

He lives—and all is well! Know self to be a part of that *living* expression of a *living* God, a *living* Creative Force, and the short arms of self will find strength in *His* awakening, *His* love, and that new commandment, "that ye love one another, would ye know the way."

Q-2. How can I understand the meaning of many of my personal qualities?
A-2. By harkening to that still small voice from within.   2741-1

The following readings, in advising a person to set an ideal, explain the steps necessary for guidance. First *consciously* seek the answer by all methods and means available, then turn to the inner consciousness.

This reading also points up the necessity for each soul to take the responsibility for helping himself.

Q-18. How can we find the true ideal?
A-18. Only that which answers to that within self can to that soul be the true ideal.

Q-19. Environment changes, or feelings, so often that it is difficult to distinguish between our environment and our ideal.
A-19. This may be to each soul a true answer for that which may be chosen in *any* manner. First seek an answer consciously for any question within thine own environ, thine own surroundings, and let thine own development, thine own ideas, answer yes and no. Then take the answer—yes or no—to the inner consciousness and let thy ruling influence in the Spirit answer. And ye may know, and the truth in same sets you free. For, when one is used by the environs that make for a questioning within self as to its ideal, know the ideal is questioned—even by the better self. Let the answer be in the highest—mental, and then in the spirit itself from within.

Q-20. Can you help me to help myself?
A-20. No soul may help another except as to that which may aid in aiding to find its own self and its relation to the Creative influences in that entity's, soul's, experience.   443-3

One person was told that so much had been accomplished in the past by reliance on divine guidance, that there were not many lives adversely affecting the current life.

As to the appearances in the earth, these have not been so many in number that aid or cause disturbances in the present. For, much has been accomplished by the entity in the turning within for the divine guidance.

Trust not any influence that denies the Sonship or His coming into the earth!   1614-2

The question is bound to arise as to how to tell when the guidance is actually divine, and not the result of wishful thinking.

Q-5. In her daily life, is she able to discriminate between the divine guidance and that of desire?

A-5. Every one may answer self in this. As He has so oft given, if ye will be silent—even though a moment—ye know. For it is not in the storm, nor in the rage, nor the tempest—but in the still small voice.　　　　903-24

Most important is what we do about any information we receive. It is necessary to set an ideal, and live up to it.

These are the characteristics that one finds with this entity. As to what the entity does *about* such is the problem, is the living experience of the entity. Thus the necessity of each entity, as for this entity, to have an ideal—and then live up to that ideal; not only in the material plane but in the mental and spiritual consciousness also.

Know what ye believe and the author of thy belief; knowing, or being persuaded by thine own consciousness, that the ideal—spiritual, mental or material—is able to keep self, to keep that, to keep the way that will lead to the closer relationship to God, in Christ-Jesus.　　　　1460-2

This was restated in the question period.

Q-5. Am I very psychic, and should I attempt to develop abilities in this direction?

A-5. As indicated. This depends upon the use to which such would be put, or the purpose to which these unfoldments would come.　　　　1460-2

Turn within, then *heed* what is given, one person was told.

Q-1. In what manner should I develop my psychic abilities?

A-1. In that which is found by turning the introspection into self, in the *light* of self's experience in the relationships *with* the developing periods throughout earth's sojourns. As this:

In the experience first there was set an ideal in the relationships of man, as man, with the Creative influences.

In the second, as the relationships of the *application* of those influences in the experiences of individuals.

In the next is seen the *determinations* to hold true, though faltering in those influences.

Again is seen the mis-interpretation of self, and the physical and mental persecutions through same.

Then, turn to that within; and *through* that; then when the Voice speaks to self within, *heed* that given.　　　　267-1

The divine spirit is the gift of the Creator in each person. Meditation and prayer are the way to realize it.

Q-2. Please explain what was meant by seeking universal source as contact for helping self and others.

A-2. Seeking the Spirit, or the *continuity* of Life *within* self, which *is* the gift *of* the Creative Force in the experience of every entity!

Q-3. Outline in detail how I should go about the development of self to make this possible in the highest manner?

A-3. By meditation and prayer in the name of that held as highest to the influences to the Throne itself; for in the *training* of the inner self may those *attunements* come—even as there is seen manifested in the mental experience those intonations that make for the influences upon the impulses, the influences upon the inner life, are controlled by the gentler, the more delicate tones, rather than the harsh.   267-1

The seeking for the highest guidance should not be reserved.

Speak oft to the *inner* self, *there* seeking for the growth, the knowledge, the understanding; and there will be made manifest in material things that growth *thou* hast made.   705-2

Setting the highest ideal, meditating, and applying spiritual truths in daily life are essential instructions.

Q-3. What is the exact means or method by which I can consciously reach the divine power or psychic force that is within me and draw upon it for the knowledge, strength, power and direction to accomplish great deeds that will bring about desired ends?

A-3. This lies latent, of course, within self. First find deep within self that purpose, that ideal to which ye would attain. Make that ideal one with thy purpose in Him. Know that within thine own body, thine own temple, He—thy Lord, thy Master—has promised to meet thee. Then as ye turn within, meditate upon those promises from body-mind (which is the soul and the mental self, or the Father *and* the Son in activity), so that there arises that consciousness of the at-onement with Him. And there may come—yea, there will come—those directions: by that constant communion with Him. *Use* this, practice this in thy daily dealings with thy fellow man; not as one that would make himself *above* his brother, but even as the Master, who made Himself one *with* His brethren, that He might save the more.

This will bring the abilities to meet the issues, because of thine own inner and former experiences and directions, in such ways that ye may become a might, a power—as ye have in former experiences—in meeting the needs of the hour.   2533-1

43

Service should be part of the ideal, the readings reiterated. This lady was told to study, to serve, and to keep listening.

Q-2. Please give me any suggestions desirable, from the cosmic point of view, concerning a method or procedure for improving my reception and response to spiritual concepts.

A-2. Studying to show thyself approved unto God, ye will not be mocked; rightly dividing and divining the words of truth; keeping self unspotted from the world. Let thy prayer be, consistently and often: "God, use me in a service to others." Let that be meaningful in thy experience, and not that some other influence guide thee, save that which is of His making, from day to day.

Q-3. Do I have the capacity for developing clairvoyance; if so, through what suggested method?

A-3. By the closing of self to the physical consciousness, and letting the universal consciousness flow through thy mind, thy body, thy soul; surrounding self with the awareness of His abiding presence with thee, ever.

Q-5. Should I drop this effort while the present opposition continues to prevent its full development?

A-5. Better keep on listening, but within—rather than giving the full expression of same; until there is the awareness as to the better means and manners of using same daily as a constructive experience at this time.   967-3

An impressive example of acting on inner guidance was reported by Dr. George Hollins, an orthopedic surgeon, in an article "The Beneficial Aspects of Meditation." (*The A.R.E. Journal,* January 1971)

"It has been my personal experience to have seen some occasions of spiritual healing. I do not feel that I have yet unfolded to the stage of being a channel for direct spiritual healing except in one or two cases, which were psychosomatic in origin and lasted for only a short time; yet there certainly have been many instances of inner guidance for healing by outer means. One of the most dramatic examples was in the case of a fine elderly gentleman from the Eastern Shore, whom I saw a few months ago. He had a tremendous bone tumor growing from his femur, the upper end of the thigh bone. This had become infected and was causing him severe pain. I put him in the hospital and did a biopsy, which is to take a piece of tissue and send it to the laboratory for study and analysis. The report came back—low-grade malignancy. The orthodox, or conventional, treatment for such a thing as that is to amputate—not only the leg, but the entire pelvis on that side.

"In such cases, we doctors don't like to take the whole responsibility on ourselves, so we seek consultation, not only for advice but also for assistance in surgery. My consultant, a young general surgeon, felt that the orthodox treatment was one that should be done, but because of the patient's age I had grave doubts that he would be able to live through such an extensive procedure. The ideal treatment would be to remove the tumor from the leg, but the tumor was of such tremendous size, and was so high up that I would not be able to get a tourniquet on above it to control the bleeding. I feared severe or fatal hemorrhage, irreparable damage to the main artery to the leg, or extension of the infection into the muscles of the thigh.

"The pathologist assured me that the tumor was one that would recur only locally, and slowly at that. As time went on it became more and more imperative to do something. I turned to meditation and the Cosmic Beloved for help. In a little while a response came as an unconventional plan unfolded before my closed eyes. The key to this plan was to have the general surgical consultant make an incision up in the abdomen and put a temporary clamp on the main artery to the leg, while I made an incision in a different way from the one I had originally planned. I would then suspend the leg after surgery with the thigh straight up, so that the drainage would be down and away from the muscle.

"I discussed this plan with my partner who was going to assist me, and at first he thought it would work. The consultant still thought the orthodox treatment was better, although he finally agreed to go along with the role I planned for him, which was to clamp the main artery. The hardest part came the day before surgery was scheduled. My partner told me that he doubted that we could get the tumor out through the incision because of its huge size. (This illustrates one of the reasons why it is a good idea to keep your inner guidance to yourself because your friends are likely to talk you out of it.) In this case, because teamwork was so essential, I couldn't keep it a secret, but I did keep the source of my idea secret. I held to my inner conviction and we went ahead with the operation. Everything worked out beautifully, and afterward all three doctors (another partner helped) told me how glad they were that it had been done the way it had."

Turning over a question or a problem to the unconscious part of the mind really works. It is both trustworthy and easily learned. It involves some effort on our part: a sincere conscious effort to find the solution, prayer and meditation, and a releasing of the question, knowing that the answer will be forthcoming, and from the greatest authority.

The more such information is used and relied on, the more easily it is obtained.

The following person was advised to trust the intuitive forces. The importance of what happens during sleep was stressed.

Q-8. What can I do to keep mentally alert and to keep back any fear of failing in my ability to succeed in my new plans?

A-8. Trust more and more in the intuitive forces, that will be the directing power through that received in the meditation with thy Maker.

Q-9. Why do I go to sleep so quickly when I begin the meditation?

A-9. Perfect relaxation. There is gradually the taking hold by the inner forces, or inner powers of the body. Train, or set self to retain more and more that which is experienced through such sleep, or such loss of consciousness; for activation is taking place. Remember, the heart doesn't stop beating because you are asleep. The brain doesn't stop acting because you are asleep. Remember all forces; for sleep is as a *sense* of the whole system, and is the great recuperating force. 257-92

Those in the habit of dream study prayerfully ask for a dream and get the answer, often the same night. Some of these report that although they may not remember a specific dream on the subject, they wake up in the middle of the night, or first thing in the morning, with the answer. Immediately on waking, the conscious mind is still close to the subconscious, and many feel that impressions received at that time are more valid and trustworthy than impressions during an active and stimuli-filled day. One of the best ways to get guidance for a knotty problem is evidently to sleep on it!

A young man reported receiving important personal help:

"During the months following my divorce I found myself more and more concerned with guilt feelings and with a desire to make things right with my ex-wife. She had remarried, and I knew of no realistic way to do anything about past mistakes. Nonetheless, much of my thought was directed toward somehow making amends.

"Then I had a dream in which I met my ex-wife in a post office (she had married a mailman). I asked her to lunch, and we entered a cafeteria. Once inside, she disappeared. I looked toward the lunch line where everyone was staring expectantly toward me as if they were closing soon. I hesitated, looking around for my ex-wife. Suddenly a voice directed me, 'Serve yourself first.' I went through the line and joined my family for lunch. I saw my ex-wife at another table, but when I approached, she totally ignored me.

46

"Upon awakening I realized that the advice to 'serve myself first' was referring to my need to seek spiritual sustenance without being preoccupied with the past. I had to continue living, without regret."

Specific physical advice is exemplified in instances contributed by two young women.

"This dream occurred when I was keeping an active dream file. It made me realize that one can actually instruct the subconscious to give information. I had had three previous dreams in which skeletons were present. To me skeletons have meant death or the dying out of something in the past. When they kept appearing I decided to get firm with myself; however, this interpretation didn't seem to fit. Before retiring, I told myself I wanted no more skeletons and if that was an important symbol, then make it much clearer or forget it! That night the dream was very simple and clear. A tall glass appeared and a very large pitcher began pouring milk into it, overflowing the sides. I got the meaning—I needed more calcium."

The second woman reported:

"The doctor had told me I was critically ill and must begin treatments including a special diet immediately. That night I dreamed of scanning my eyes down the label of a giant vitamin bottle. The words 'folic acid' leaped out and filled my entire vision. A voice said: 'Remember, the body needs folic acid.' The doctor's examination the next day confirmed this need, and folic acid supplements were added to the diet."

A retired businessman reported seeking and receiving guidance on a very practical matter.

Dream 1. "I was playing a kind of poker with another man. Chips were blue with silver markings. I seemed to have a good hand and bet. My opponent called and raised. I re-raised heavily. He hesitated; waited a long time; finally called without raising. There was about $2,000 in the pot. In the dream I was thinking, 'This is great. I should make a career out of this.' Then I realized I was in a game I knew nothing whatsoever about. Dream ended without disclosing whether I won or lost."

Dream 2. "Early nighttime. I am walking down the center of a street lined on each side with Chinese gambling houses, each with lookouts sitting in little cubicles to control the doorways. (Similar to a street in Stockton, California many years ago.) One of the lookouts taps and beckons but I ignore and walk on. Then I am in a Chinese lottery parlor. The operator gives me a Chinese ink brush and shows me how to mark the ticket, since I know nothing about the procedure. There are numbered squares on both sides of the ticket and I have to check off ten preferences. I am playing just one 25¢ ticket."

Interpretations: "I had been toying with the idea of investing about $2,000 in blue chip stocks when the Dow dropped below 600. Both dreams are in response to request for guidance. Both tell me I'm getting into something about which I know nothing. Dream 2 tells me to stay in the middle—don't get involved—but then, if I do, be gentle. 25¢ is enough!"

A mother told of a dream that emphasized the availability of inner guidance, and which she said had buoyed her during a trying time.

"This happened some years ago when I was more distraught than I had ever been in my life. There was a particularly heartbreaking situation in our family at the time and I was trying to cope with it, seeking help from all kinds of sources, and trying somehow to do an efficient job at my office.

"One night when I went to bed and fell into an exhausted sleep I had one nightmare after another. Each one was an elaboration and exaggeration of the current situation. Each more horrible than the last. After each one I woke sobbing. Finally, around four in the morning I realized that if it kept up I would be a drained emotional wreck in the morning and unable to help my family at all. I prayed fervently for rest and strength.

"When I slept again, I dreamed that I was going into a second-floor lecture hall where I was to be the chairman. I was carrying a baby, a girl. The room was crowded, and as I busied myself with the necessary details I suddenly realized that I no longer had the baby. Annoyed at my carelessness in mislaying the baby, I went downstairs to see if I had left her there. I was told that I had taken the baby upstairs with me. Dashing up the steps and re-entering the hall I could hear the baby shrieking over the hubbub of the crowd. When I followed the ever-louder screaming, I found her with a young couple. The wife was trying to comfort the baby. Sensing the young woman's embarrassment and feeling of being ineffectual, I took the baby and delivered a firm lecture to her. 'There's no need for you to carry on like this,' I said. 'You know perfectly well that I wouldn't desert you. These people were trying to help you. Help was right here. It's just like the love of the Father. It's right there, if you'll only accept it.' Then, in the dream I said to myself, 'That's really very good. I must remember that.'

"When I woke from that dream, I laughed. It was so clear that the baby girl was me, the helpless baby self that I have taken with me into adulthood. All night I had had nightmares and had been crying, yet I was not alone and help was there for the accepting. In the weeks and months that ensued until the traumatic situation was resolved, if ever

I felt alone, or felt sorry for myself, I'd pull myself up and think, 'That's enough, crybaby!' and then I'd pray. Over the years the memory of that very vivid dream has sustained me and reminded me that help is closer than my right hand."

Find the answer within self. *Know* it is not by chance that the opportunities are before thee in the present. Hence studying first to know thy ideal—spiritually, mentally, materially—show thyself approved in all good conscience unto that thou hast chosen as thy ideal.

Then applying self in those directions, we should find not only harmony and success materially, but that feeling, that peace as He has promised to all who seek to know His way. · 933-3

See also:
Breakthrough to Creativity, Shafica Karagulla, M.D.
Edgar Cayce on Religion and Psychic Experience, Harmon H. Bro, Ph.D.

Chapter V

CAN I BE A MEDIUM?

Among the various kinds of psychics who are reading for people are those known as mediums, who communicate or purport to communicate with entities who are no longer living. A variety of human emotions ranging from grief, love, possessiveness and guilt keep their clientele faithful and often dependent.

Mediumship is one of the oldest of the divinatory practices, known in ancient Egypt and Greece, and reported in the Old Testament. During the Dark Ages, up to the seventeenth and eighteenth centuries, people who seemed to communicate with spirits of the dead easily became targets for torture and death. But in the nineteenth century, a semi-respectability clothed the communicators. By 1860 a craze for spirit communication began sweeping the country. Although trickery was discovered occasionally, much was accepted as genuine. Not long after the tragic death of his son, Willie, President Abraham Lincoln attended séances in the White House arranged by his grieving wife.

The Edgar Cayce readings assure us that the soul is immortal, that life is continuous, and that death is but "passing through God's other door" (5749-3). If this is true—and we all have psychic ability—should we not, in fact, be able to communicate with those who have passed on? Is it good to do so? Cayce was asked this and related questions many times.

This woman's husband had died two years previously:

Q-2. Is it well to foster the sense of continued communication with his spirit while we are separated by "death," so-called?

A-2. If this is for a helpful experience to each, it is well. Let it rather be directed by that communion with *Him* who has promised to be WITH thee always! and hinder not then thy companion, but—in such associations and meetings—give the direction to the Holy One.   1782-1

The suggestion is that to foster such communication could hinder the loved one who had died. Another widow received similar advice, with a strong influence that such "hanging on" might be selfish.

Q-1. Have I any further contact with my late husband . . . since he has passed on?

A-1. If that is the desire, it will continue to hang on to same! If it is to be finished, and that which has been to be the development, then leave this aside.

Q-2. Does he know of my prayers?

A-2. Do you wish him to? Do you wish to call him back to those disturbing forces, or do you wish the self to be poured out for him that he may be happy? Which is it you desire—to satisfy self that you are communicating, or that you are holding him in such a way as to retard? or hast thou BELIEVED the promise? Leave him in the hands of Him who is the resurrection! Then prepare thyself for same. 1786-2

Another woman asked in a reading that Cayce be used as a medium to contact her deceased husband. She was told that such communication should be spontaneous, and was reminded that although the husband was dead, the transition had not changed the soul's problems. The source refused to try to contact the individual.

Mrs. C: You will have before you the body and enquiring mind of [610], present in this room, in regard to the problems in her life at the present time, and her desire to communicate with her husband . . . who passed from this earth plane on March 27, 1933. If possible, we seek to make this contact. You will give any advice and guidance that will be helpful to her, answering the questions that may be asked.

Mr. C: Yes, we have the body, the enquiring mind, [610], present in this room, with the problems and the conditions that confront and disturb this body at this time.

While it is possible for the body, to receive communication from . . . this should be rather through self than *any* other channel. While he . . . is present with the body, [610], now, for the communications that he would give it is best that these be their very own; for these are rather as they have been during the experience of their sojourn in the earth. To use this channel here would be to lessen the abilities in many directions. There may be received much respecting that which may be given from the universal sources, rather than individual. For, each soul should know, because the body has laid aside the shell, because the soul has been released from those bonds, those taxations of the material things, this has not changed the problems of any soul. They are—as knowledge, as truth, as understanding—a *growth* in those things that have and do become problems for the mental body of any entity.

In this, then, if the body seeks for those things that may be given from that source, well. If it seeks the individual, then we would advise choosing other channels. 610-1

That contact and communication could be spontaneous was revealed in a number of questions triggered by such occurrences. The readings offered the surprising advice that it was the departed entities who needed help and prayer in most instances.

Q-1. The entity has had the experience of awaking at night and feeling the presence of her brother—would appreciate an explanation of this.
A-1. This is a reality.
Q-2. On June 2, 1942, the entity heard her brother calling her—was this the exact time that he passed on?
A-2. Not the exact time, but when the entity could—and found the attunement such as to speak with thee.
Q-3. Was there something he wanted her to know?
A-3. Much that he needs of thee. Forget not to pray for and with him; not seeking to hold him but that he, too, may walk the way to the light, in and through the experience. For this is well. Those who have passed on need the prayers of those who live aright. For the prayers of those who would be righteous in spirit may save many who have erred, even in the flesh. 3416-1

The dead need our prayers to help them on the other side.

Q-5. Please explain the seeming communications I have had from Harold Lockwood, an actor who died in 1918, whom I never knew in life.
A-5. As self is a "sensitive," at times, and as Lockwood and others seek expression, these oft become close to the borderline. Ye may help Lockwood by thy prayer, that he be released from the earthbound hope. 2783-1

Q-9. From time to time I have had to come into my room a friend who has passed on. Is this contact harmful or beneficial?
A-9. In this, there are always those seeking that we may help, that may help us; for as we help another does help come to us. Pray for that friend, that the way through the shadows may be easier for them. It becomes easier for you. 262-25

We draw them to us, and we should pray that the Father guide them.

Q-2. It seems that some entity, perhaps an Indian guide, has sought on various occasions to come through to me. Please explain this.
A-2. Is it any wonder, with the gentleness, kindness, the patience shown in the experiences just before this, that the entity should seek to counsel with

thee? These seek rather not to do other than gain from thee knowledge as to the application of right and justice.

Then when these approach, let thy counsel be, "The Father direct thee, the Father guide thee, the Father bless thee."

These will make for, then, the abilities for the awakening to come along the line for those who are seeking—seeking for further expressions! and their advancement then may be quickly accomplished through this veil that ye see only darkly at times.   1610-2

One person questioned the effect of a discarnate friend on her, and was reminded that the communications came to her only as assurances, not as guidance. To accept help from less than the highest source, God the Father, would only bring confusion. George dead was not any wiser or all-knowing than George living.

Q-7. How much effect does George . . . [deceased son of 1210] have on my thinking and do you find his directions as helpful for me as for his father?

A-7. Only to that extent as ye allow him to have an effect!

Who is thy God? Who is thy Way? In Whom do ye live and move?

Is not the Father in Jesus Christ the Lord of all? Is He not God of the living, whether they be in spirit, in mind or in body?

Then why *question* ye? These communications come as *assurances*, not as guides, not as directors! For He *alone* is the Way! He *alone* is the Truth!

Then *why—why* harken to that which will *only* bring confusion, when ye confuse thy ideal?   954-5

This advice was reiterated in the following answer, stressing that souls who were held to the earth plane as spirit guides were hindered in their development.

Q-7. Stewart Hoover who is in the spirit world—is he the one who guides me and should I cultivate the relationship?

A-7. This is not amiss, but best not for cultivation; else ye limit thyself and hinder Stewart Hoover in his real development.

For, remember, the Father, God, hath promised to meet thee in thy temple. Thy body is the temple of the living God. Thy body is as the shadow of the tabernacle, and He will meet thee in the holy of holies. Remember, as thy Master, thy Lord, thy Christ has given, "I stand at the door and knock, and if ye will open I will enter and abide with thee—I and the Father." This as ye conceive, this as ye understand, is the highest source of understanding, of knowledge. And it is the self that seeks this understanding, this comprehension—not at the expense of another, but in that manner in which ye may aid even those who are in the inter-between, who having not here gained the full concept are still in that position even as He gave in the parable, "If they hear not Moses and the prophets, they would not listen though one appeared from the dead."

Hence these are as the greater openings for thyself. Think it not robbery to make thyself equal with God, for He is thy Father. Then approach Him in thy inner self as ye would thy earthly father, with that same conviction that He heareth and will answer thee—and that *thou* usest that understanding in thy relationships with thy fellow man!

For as He gave, "As ye do it unto the least of thy brethren, ye do it unto thy Maker."

So when there are little jealousies, little hates, little selfishnesses, ye are hindering, ye are wounding the conscience, the love of the Father as manifests in thee. And His commandment is ever, "Love one another."

1581-2

Yet when discarnate loved ones are drawn to us spontaneously, there are times when both may gain from the strength and love.

Q-1. Does the spirit of my father ever hover around his family, and—

A-1. Oft, as the self has felt that abiding strength, through those periods when there seemed no end to the discontent as about self, does the body know and feel that spirit guiding, aiding, strengthening; for, as He has given, "He will give His angels charge concerning thee, lest thou unwittingly dash thy foot against a stone." As the spirit of power and strength of those about us gain in their activity, through the allowing of self to dwell upon the truths given in our mental being, so are *they* enabled to give strength to our faltering material selves.

2118-1

This lady [1376] seemed to have been experimenting with mediumship. Her question mentioned "controls," and she was told firmly that to be controlled or directed by another entity was to give up her free will. In a later question she asked how to protect herself and was told to call on the Christ.

Q-3. Are the methods recommended by her controls the proper ones for securing financial support which is needed?

A-3. "There is today set before thee good and evil, life and death—Choose thou!"

As we find, to be controlled or directed by an *entity* that has not proclaimed—Well, it is allowing will to be broken.

Do today the things thy hands, thy mind, thy body, find to do. Put thyself either in the hands of the I AM THAT I AM—or of the I AM that would seek

54

first for self to be eased, or for self to be freed—or the earthly things and not the heavenly, the Godly.

Q-4. Are the entities who present themselves as guides for [1376] the persons they represent themselves to be and how far may their suggestions be followed for her best development?

A-4. Such questions are answered when those purposes, those desires have been determined within the inmost self of [1376].

How spoke he when he wrestled with the evil one regarding the physical body of Moses? Read that portion of Jude in which this is given.

Be ye not as the winds that blow about, as clouds without water; but be ye steadfast in the word of truth . . .

Q-8. Please explain how she may protect herself from these entities?

A-8. As an entity, a soul, a mind, enters—as has been so oft given—put about the self the cloak, the garment, yea the mantle of *Christ;* not as a man, not as an individual but the Christ—that universal consciousness of love that we see manifested in those who have forgotten self but—*as* Jesus—give themselves that others may know the truth.

For the promise has been, "If ye will call, I will *hear!*" "If ye will call, I *will hear!*"

That is the protection. Call—that the spirit of truth, that is manifested in the promises of an *All*-Loving Father, be about self in the seeking to aid, to bring cheer, hope, help, faith, courage to the weak, to the discouraged, to the disconsolate. These be the promises—and how hath it been said? "Though the heavens and the earth pass away, my words, my promises shall *not*"—unless ye supersede them by the promises of man!   1376-1

As in all kinds of guidance, we must choose the highest, the best.

Q-7. Who is my spirit teacher, "Amicus," and how may I best cooperate and keep in touch with him?

A-7. Read that as has been given. If ye choose less than the full creative forces, thy Maker, ye fall short of thy abilities.   2021-1

One problem with consulting mediums, according to the readings, was a question of interpretation. At times messages alleged to be from the other side were simply from the subconscious mind of the individual. Difficulty in interpretation meant that often information thus obtained, though not deliberately false, was not necessarily true.

Q-30. Is the medium Buddy, friend of my friend Clara in Washington, reliable or false?

A-30. This as we find is to be determined by individuals who seek information through such channels. There *are* through mediumships various interpretations by the sources from which such information comes. For, as we have indicated through this channel heretofore, oft there are those sources that are purely of the subconscious mind of the individual entity. At other periods there are the interpretations, or attempts to read from those records that are a part of the universal forces; and in the intent to interpret such there may be many misleading interpretations and directions taken, from that attempted to be given.

Not intentionally false, but not always true.   1947-5

Seek not other entities! This excerpt, while admitting that there are discarnates about, says that there is a "communion of sinners" as well as of saints!

Q-2. Give me any specific guidance in developing the pattern indicated above, which may be helpful at this point.

A-2. None better than that as we have outlined. Know it is within self, and it is found—the manner of approach—in the 30th of Deuteronomy, and in the 14th, 15th, 16th and 17th of John. Not that other approaches may not be just as important, just as beautiful—but here the directions are crystallized into that of knowing thine own body is the temple. It is thy tabernacle. There He will meet thee.

Seek not other entities. Not that many are not about; not that there is not the communion of saints, but there is also the communion of sinners! Ye seek not those!

Let that light be in thee which was also in the Christ Jesus, who went about *doing* good! bearing His cross, as ye must indeed bear thy cross, but bearing it in Him it brings peace, and most of all life everlasting, and hope and cheer!

Be not longfaced, but happy—*happy*—in thy service to others.   2787-1

The information in these readings convincingly states that although it is possible to develop mediumistic abilities, it is most unwise. It involves surrendering the soul's birthright, the free will, to another entity. Depending on help from another entity who has passed on retards both parties.

Q-2. Do I have psychic and mediumistic powers?

A-2. As has been indicated, all forms and natures of same may manifest through the entity.

As to the branch that may be chosen, THIS is to be determined by the entity—when it has analyzed itself.

Q-3. Do I need training and further guidance other than that which I receive through myself?

A-3. Thy body is the temple. *There* He hath promised to meet thee. Be not overcome by others, but overcome in HIS name—Christ's name!

Q-4. In what ways have I pursued such activities in former incarnations?

A-4. As indicated, in the manner in which there was the preparation—in the vision, in the activities, and in the directing of others in other appearances.

Q-5. Any advice as to what form of mediumship I should use?

A-5. Rather this should be, as indicated:

"FATHER-GOD! HERE AM I—USE ME; NOT AS *I* WILL, BUT AS THOU SEEST IS THE MANNER IN WHICH I MAY BETTER SERVE *THY* PURPOSE WITH MAN!" 2425-1

Ideals and purposes are an integral part of development. The use of any psychic ability for selfish or material purposes is to the individual's undoing.

Through thine undertakings, through thine experiences ye have been and are endowed with an intuition that becomes what ye term psychic force in thy abilities, in thy powers. If thy soul's abilities are being expended for the gratifying of a material desire, they come to naught. If they are expressed and manifested in such ways and manners as to be to the glory of the Father, to the understanding of thy brethren that they may know the love the Father beareth the children of men, then indeed shall they grow and bring forth sixty, yea, an hundred fold—in what? "My peace I leave with you—not as the world giveth peace, but my peace I give unto you"—you that *use,* you that *apply* that power of God in thyself through thy intuition, yea through thy soul force, that thy visions, thy dreams, yea thy powers make thee walk with God! Yet if ye do these for that of lauding or lording thy knowledge, thy abilities over the humblest, yea the greatest, yea the vilest of thy acquaintances, ye do so to thine own confusion, thine own undoing. 1440-2

Without a strong spiritual ideal, there can be uncertainty and confusion, and there is certainly no guarantee of perfection:

... in the occult, in the spiritual phenomena, in the activities that bind the entity to the universal consciousness. These are well if balanced, but there are extremes when doubts and fears arise. Know that there are those realms wherein there is as much confusion as there is in the material world, unless the ideal that is ever creative in its purpose is the directing influence. 3617-1

When would mediumship be a benefit, then?

Beware of mysteries that may not be practical in material experiences, but beware as much of those that would make their soul or psychic experiences so practical as to become null to the spiritual attitude or development of a soul itself. For, the spirit *is* the association—or the life itself of the soul, whether in man, in a nation, in a city, in a group, or what. For, the activities that count to every soul are the unseen forces that may *not* be measured in the crucible nor may they be taped by any meter. As the hart panteth after the water, so may the soul pant for the garden of the spiritual and spirit influence of its betters.   476-1

Every soul has the ability to accomplish any influence that has been or may be accomplished in the earth. It is dependent on the ideal. (See also 3083-1, Ch. I)

Direct communication with loved ones who have passed on is often spontaneously present in dreams. Mutual love and mutual desire for communication seem to be the controlling factors. Many families who have no belief at all in psychic phenomena tell stories of such dreams. Often while they realize the very real solace brought in this way, they fail to understand the reality that dreams of this sort demonstrate— the reality that life is continuous, that the entity withdrawn from the physical body exists in another dimension of consciousness.

One woman, born late in her mother's life, grieved almost to the point of illness when her mother passed on. She had lived all of her life, even after marriage, with her mother and they had been unusually close. Some time after the mother's death, when she slept, she heard her mother talking to her. "Don't keep crying, Lillian. Everything is all right. If only I could explain it to you—I'm close to you. It's just as if there's a thin veil between us." From that time, Lillian felt at peace about her mother and able to cope with her family and daily life. Was it simply a wish fulfilled by the mind? The readings emphasize the fact that such communication is both possible and real.

Q-1. Does the communication between those who have passed into the spirit plane and those on the earth depend on previously established relationships, on understanding and love, or upon what?

A-1. "As the tree falleth so will it lie." Because there are changes in the dimensional conditions does not alter that which is known in the earth plane as desire. If the desire is in that direction that there may be an association with, an aid to, a seeking of such associations, then only the means, the channel, the way, the course, is necessary to complete the communication.

The attunement of that materially known as the radio may offer an illustration for this. If there is the desire that the communication be with those from plane to plane, the attunement of an individual in the material or earth plane to the attunement of the entity in the spirit or fourth-dimensional plane is necessary. Remember the first premise, "As the tree falleth so does it lie." If there is the desire on the part of those in the spirit or fourth-dimensional plane to be communicated with, and the same element of desire is attuned from another plane, stratum, sphere or condition, then such may be done; hence, it may truly be said that *all* factors have their influence, desire the ruling one; and the desire must be attuned to the same vibration of the one in another plane, as the radio; for who of those seeking would seek His Face must know, believe, that He is, attuning their abilities, their efforts, in that direction, acting, feeling, knowing, that there *is* the response.   5756-8

Another lady reported dreaming of her stepfather years after his death. She felt the dream offered reinforcement to her.

"I dreamed I was lying in bed and as I looked out of the window, I saw my beloved stepfather's face come into view. (He had passed over in 1941.) His expression was one of radiant pleasure, a broad, beaming, illuminated smile. No words were spoken. In his earth-life, my stepfather had been a deeply spiritual person although as a child I did not recognize this aspect of him.

"This dream conveyed to me that he was very pleased that I had at last found the spiritual path on which I was deeply and seriously embarked."

In the readings are many examples of communication. The following excerpt shows precognition which was to serve as a warning. Attunement made it possible.

Q-1. One recent morning. Saw my mother. She told me that I should warn my Aunt Helen against an accident. Helen seemed to get into an accident, get badly hurt, and my mother took sick from it.

A-1. This, as is presented, is an accident regarding getting injured in an automobile and street car accident. Be warned, then, and warn the body as regarding same, see? and when the body keeps in that way of being warned, or keeps from the car, then this may not be expected to happen, for here we have, as it were, the direct communication of the entity in the spirit plane with the entity in the material plane, the attunement being reached when the entity in the body-conscious mind being subjugated and an at-onement with universal forces. This also shows the entity how that the entity in the spirit plane, or spirit entity, is mindful of conditions which transpire, exist, in the material plane, see?

Q-2. When is this accident in danger of happening to my Aunt Helen?

A-2. Within the present moon's phase, for that is as that element bringing those conditions to bear regarding the body—the universality again of the elements, and their action or activity, or relativity of forces, regarding individuals in the earth's plane. Before the waning of the moon, see?

Q-3. In what manner?

A-3. As given, street car and automobile accident.

Q-4. How may it be avoided?

A-4. As given. Be warned of riding in either through these phases—that is, until the waning of the moon.   136-48

Several years ago, a salesman on his way to work was killed when the car he was driving crashed into an overpass. He had an excellent driving record with no history of accidents or recklessness. In good health, he was on no medication. Police found no evidence of any other car, nor were there any witnesses. His family was at a loss to understand how the tragedy had happened. Within a week after his untimely passing, his widow dreamed about him. In the dream he explained that there had been another car involved. It had careened toward him in the wrong lane, and he had swerved to avoid it.

Dream studies are filled with dramatic case reports in which those who have crossed over seem to return to their loved ones with information and help that only they can provide. Such communication is safe and natural.

The readings show that communication can also take place by means of thought impressions. If this is done it is necessary that a person be well balanced, physically healthy, and guided by an ideal of service.

Also we will find that, with the attunement of the self in the periods when the body sits for that of the silence, the better *physically* fit the better the *attunement* will be for those active forces of the psychic influences, and of the connective ratios between the Borderland and the Beyond for the entity; for, as has been given, the voices may be heard by this body when *attuning* self, even as the *vision and* the voice. Keep self attuned. Keep in that way and manner as befitting *that* as is *desired* by the body, for first there is the desire—then there is the proper seeking for that desired. Not as selfish motives, but that self may aid even those *in* the Borderland in their understanding of the relationships of an entity *to* its creative forces, and that which the *soul* seeks. Amen.   599-8

The following dream is an example of a communication dream which also shows clairvoyance in a dream. The lady who had it felt that it was given to her so that she could pray for her daughter and for the soul who would choose to be born to her.

"I was dreaming—I dreamed that I saw my mother and some of my other relatives who had passed over. All were sitting on chairs in a circle out on a beautiful lawn. As I approached I heard a voice say, 'Did you all know that Jeanne was pregnant again?' Jeanne is my daughter and it was her grandmother who said it. I was so shocked, all I could say was 'What!' When I said that, all turned and looked in my direction. Somebody said, 'We didn't intend for you to hear that.'

I became visibly disturbed. Her baby, John Thomas, was only four months old and there were two other children.

"For days I kept telling myself that it was only a dream and to stop thinking about it. On Sunday afternoon I could stand it no longer, so I put a long distance call in for Washington, D.C., where she lived. My daughter answered the phone; I put the question bluntly to her. She answered, 'No, Mother, nothing like that!' We chatted awhile and then hung up. I felt relieved, but not for long. In a few days I received a letter from her. She wrote, 'Mother, I couldn't talk to you Sunday when you called because I had guests. I am pregnant, but how in the world did you know? I haven't told a soul.'

"From that time on I prayed for my child and her unborn baby."

We can help those who have crossed over by praying for them. When we think of them or dream of them our prayer should be that they go toward the Light.

For every individual entity knows himself better than any other. Be sincere with yourself and other outside influences, even disincarnate entities with and through whom ye may obtain much, will be sincere with you. Sincerity will drive away those that might hinder, but do not use them, do not abuse them. Know that these come to thee for aid, not to aid you. Aid them! Thus are we admonished to pray for the dead. Pray for the dead, for they only sleep—as the Lord indicated. And if we are able to attune to such, there we may help. Though we may not call back to life as the Son, we can point the way. For there's only one way. And point to that, that is safe in Him, who is the way, the truth and the light.   3657-1

See also:
Human Personality and Its Survival of Bodily Death, F.W.H. Myers
The Belief in a Life After Death, C. Ducasse, Ph.D.
God's Other Door, Hugh Lynn Cayce
During Sleep, Robert Crookall, B.Sc., Ph.D.

Chapter VI

WHAT IS MY PURPOSE?

What am I doing here? Where am I going? More important, after some self-evaluation, where should I be going? These questions which often identify the person who has started soul searching are among those that psychics are asked regularly.

The Edgar Cayce readings have much to say about the purpose for an entity's incarnation. Contrary to what one might expect there was not a wide variety of advice in this information, and all of it was closely linked to the forming of, and working toward, an ideal. The emphasis was on man's creation in the image of the Creator and his heritage of free will.

An entity, or soul, is a spark—or a portion—of the Whole, the First Cause; and thus is a co-worker with that First Cause, or Purpose, which is the creative influence or force that is manifested in materiality.

Each entity, each soul, is endowed with self-will; that which is the force that makes it able, or gives it the capacity, to be the law, and yet complying with a universal purpose.

Thus, whether the activities or consciousnesses are in the material expression or in the universal cosmic expression in the spirit, these are ever a part of the entity's expression—for either development or retardment.

As may be seen, then, the activites or entrances of an entity into materiality and out of materiality are not so much governed by the stars or planets as they are by what the entity has done respecting the law of its relationships to same!

Thus it may be said, as the entity or soul—a soul—is part of the Creative Forces, the positions of the stars or planets do not influence the entity so much as the entity has influenced, and does influence, the affairs of a universal consciousness! . . .

For, indeed each entity, each soul, is in the process of evolution towards the First Cause. Much becomes evolution—much may become involution.

2079-1

The purpose of each soul is to become a channel for universal consciousness and to express that consciousness in his relationships with his fellow man. The highest spiritual ideal must be made a vital and living part of the experience.

For each soul enters for a purposefulness, that it may be a channel through which this universal consciousness—that is ever present, and being sought as it were by the inmost forces of the entity—may be seen, may find expression in the experience of the fellow man.

As in the studies of the entity it is seen that the soul of man is a mere speck in space, yet the soul—though indefinite—is that vital force or activity which is everlasting. Though the earth, though the stars, may pass away; though there may be changes in the universe as to the relative position, these are brought about by those combinations of that speck of human activity as relative *to* the soul's expression in any sphere of experience.

This then is an experience for the entity in which there may be the application of self in its relationships to others, in giving expression of that which is its ideal, its standard; not for self but for that it, the entity, the soul, would worship in its Maker, its Creator.

It is not sufficient that there be a reverence but that—as is held as an active principle in the mental mind, the spiritual mind of the entity—such an ideal must be a practical experience of each and every soul. And this one experiences in that it prompts that entity, that soul, to apply in relationships to its fellow men.   1297-1

How can this be accomplished? The next excerpt outlines the steps, with a special stress on the fruits of the spirit. The mission and purpose for this person were not to go to some far-flung place to get started, but rather to be a witness for the Lord to those he met, day by day.

Then, as ye show forth the fruits of the spirit. What are these? Faith, hope, patience, long-suffering, kindness, gentleness, brotherly love—these be those over which so many stumble; yet they are the very voices, yea the very morning sun's light in which the entity has caught that vision of the *New Age*, the new understanding, the new seeking for the relationships of a Creative Force to the sons of men.

And indeed then the purposes are to manifest in such measures those fruits that they who are weak take hope, they who have faltered gain new courage, they who are disappointed and disheartened gain a new concept of hope that springs eternally within the human breast.

For God is not mocked, and whatsoever a man soweth, that shall he also reap.

Remember above all, as He hath given, "As ye do it unto the least of thy brethren, of thy associates, of thy companions, day by day, ye do it unto thy God; yea, the God within *thyself!*

For unless the answer is "My spirit beareth witness with that which is my hope for life, my conception of eternity, my conception of life that is *Thy* conception"—unless it beareth witness with these, ye are indeed wandering far afield. But His promises have been, "Seek and ye shall find; knock and it shall be opened unto thee."

And these become then thy mission. Open the door for those that cry aloud for a knowledge that God is within the reach of those that will put their hand to *doing;* just being kind—not a great deed as men count greatness, but just being gentle and patient and loving even with those that would despitefully use thee. For the beauties of the Lord are with those that seek to know and *witness* for Him among men.

That is thy mission, that is thy purpose, in this material experience.

What then is the mental attitude to be? In keeping with that which has been given, "Lo Lord, I am thine—to be directed as *Thou*—not my fellow man, but *Thou*—would direct."

For He hath given His angels charge concerning thee, that ye faint not by the way. For He stands—*stands*—at the door and knocks, and if ye will open He will come and sup with thee. For He *is* life and light and immortality; and the way is good.   1436-1

Knowledge and understanding will result if one's purposes, desires and meditations are in accord with what one knows to do. Throughout the readings is the often repeated idea that what counts is what one *does* with the knowledge one has. Most important is knowing oneself, according to the readings. The next step is the setting of an ideal. The following selection illustrates that only in the application of the fruits of the spirit can any soul learn its true purpose.

In choosing the interpretations of the records to be given here, this is done with the hope and desire that the entity may indeed apply that which has been given of old, "Know Thyself."

And in the analysis of this, and the seeking to apply that which is good, know that these are chosen from a standard—an ideal.

Know then that an ideal, physical, mental and spiritual, must be a part of the experience of each, if there would be a gaining, a developing, a fulfilling of the purposes for which each soul enters a material experience.

For there is the constant meeting of self in the varied experiences, and we are the result of all we have been in respect *to* that which is the ideal, the way, the truth and the light.

It is only in the application of these, that are the fruits of the spirit, that each soul may indeed come to know that purpose for which it enters a given experience.   1500-3

There is no need to rely on others to tell us what problems we are here to work on; all we need to do is to look at ourselves honestly and examine our shortcomings.

Q-1. How can I shape my life so as to make the greatest possible spiritual advancement in this incarnation?

A-1. Study those things that have been the shortcomings, and those that have been and that have brought the greater blessings in the experiences through the various sojourns in the earth. Then magnify those things in which there is greater stress, and greater faith, and greater activity toward bringing material as well as mental and spiritual development. They are—as has been set—ever the same. For the law of the Lord *is* perfect, converting the soul. It reneweth a righteous spirit within thee, day by day. Meditate oft, then, in those things and in those experiences.

For, much of that which was the activity through those various periods, by thy own intuitive force, may be made better known to thee; and as to how and in what manner ye may conduct self, not only in relationships to others but as to conditions which arise in the experience of those ye meet day by day.

Remember to keep that appreciativeness, not only for what He is, has been and ever will be in thy experience, but that ye may *glorify* Him in thy speech, in thy activity, in thy associations one with another.

Q-2. Have I any psychic abilities which can be developed for the good of myself and others?

A-2. As has just been indicated, these have extended, do extend, deep into the *intuitive* forces—from the very beginning. But find the answer deep within self. For, as given—self, thy body, thy mind, thy soul, is the seat of thy relationship, thy association, thy connection with thy Maker—even thy Elder Brother, who has promised to meet thee within thine own temple. Then, meditate oft therein, as ye allow that consciousness to arise through thine own body, in the emotions as will come by the closer thought along this line:

I AM GOD'S OWN. THROUGH ME HAS COME MANY GENERA-TIONS OF THOUGHT, OF MANIFESTATION. SHOW ME, O GOD, THE WAY.

And then, as ye listen, there will come that assurance, that help, that understanding as to what, as to how those activities are to find material expression in the present. For He changeth not.

Then, rely not upon others. For, as was the pronouncement of old, it is not who will come and give thee a message; for, lo, as has been indicated, thou art from the beginning of the manifestations of God's love. Then magnify same, listen, be patient; for in patience ye become aware of thy soul, and its relationship to Him. 1857-2

The young woman who requested the following reading was particularly interested in advice about the development of her psychic abilities in service to others. The beginning of the reading describes creation, and goes on to explain that all of creation is "bound in the consciousness of self," and that creative force is the psychic self. The purpose of entrance into materiality is to develop body, mind and soul to the glory of Creative Force. Only by self-centeredness and losing sight of that purpose can an entity be hindered. The reading points to the universal laws that govern this growth.

The body finds itself Body, Mind and Soul; the body with all its attributes, with the mental and material and physical desires and emotions; the mental with its hopes and fears, its aspirations and desires; the spiritual with its longings, its wonderments, its interpreting of the emotions of physical and mental being.

These, then, in the light of all that has been indicated, should be analyzed, and then the premise from which the ideal is to be drawn; and how same works with the *entity* as an entity.

It has already been indicated in the information given that the entity has abilities in certain directions, partaking of the mental and spiritual or soul forces; as well as much to be met in the physical emotions.

Mind is the builder; it is both spiritual and physical, and thus has its aspirations, its limitations, its fears, its hopes, its desires.

To determine, then, whether the emotions or influences which arise from one experience to another are from purely a mental aspiration of a physical desire, or from a spiritual aspect and hope in its relationships to the things desired of self—comparisons need to be drawn for the entity as to how, and in what manner judgments or choices are to be made.

The body finds itself Body, Mind, Soul; just as seen in that after which it is patterned—Father, Son, Holy Spirit.

In the choices, then, it is seen that each of these phases of spiritual experience finds its own place of activity, as illustrated in the entity's experience in materiality.

The *Spirit* moved—or soul moved—and there was Light (Mind). The Light became the light of men—Mind made aware of conscious existence in spiritual aspects or relationships as one to another.

The mind in the entity becomes aware of longings, innate in the inner self; also the arousing of emotions in the physical attributes of the body—just as indicated as to how these came into *being;* as self is a part of Creative Forces or God, Spirit, the Son. These are one. The body, mind and soul are one. Their desires must be one; their purposes, their aims must be one—then—to be ideal.

What, then, has this to do with the entity in its seeking for the use of its own abilities in the psychic, the mental, the material atmosphere in which it finds itself in the present?

There are laws, then, as govern the physical, the mental, the spiritual body, and the attributes of each of these. The abuse of a physical law brings dis-ease and then disturbance to the physical organism, through which mental and spiritual portions of the body operate.

There are also promises, warnings, and governing forces, as has been indicated, for the physical and the mental and spiritual being—as given by those forces and influences which manifest in the material world as respecting each of these.

As the Mind indicated, "I and the Father are one; he that abideth in me as I abide in the Father *hath* eternal life." Not *will* have, not *may* have, but *hath*—now—is in eternal consciousness of being at a onement with eternal influence and force!

And this is the moving of the spirit that has brought and does bring life, light, to the consciousness of the entity in whatever phase of experience it may be passing.

Then how, in what manner, does one accomplish such? Not by thoughts of self. If God had not given free will to man, or the children of men, would they have been able to be equal with Him? Rather would they be as the natural sources of the universal consciousness of group vibration—as is indicated about the entity.

"Be not deceived," then, it was given, "God is not mocked; whatsoever a man soweth, that must he also reap."

Then, not merely by *doing* does the awareness come, but by *being in* the doing does the awareness come of the relationships as one portion of body, mind and soul finds.

These then grow, as indicated, as do individuals. This entity as an entity grows in grace, in knowledge, in understanding.

As was indicated, the body was first a cell by the union of desire that brought activity in that influence about which the growth began.

Then of itself at birth into materiality the consciousness gradually awoke to the influences about same of body, mind and soul, until it reached the consciousness of the ability for the reproduction within itself of desire, hope, fear.

And the whole of creation, then, is bound in the consciousness of self. That influence, that force is the psychic self.

As to how same, then, may be developed within self:

Each entity enters materiality for a purpose. That all the experiences in the earth are as one is indicated by the desires, the longings as arise within the experience of that which makes for the growing, the knowing within self—MIND! Thus does the entity, as a whole, become aware that it, itself, in body, mind and soul, is the result—each day—of the application of laws pertaining to creation, this evolution, this soul-awareness within, consciously manifested.

What is the purpose of entering consciousness? That each phase of body, mind and soul may be to the glory of that Creative Force in which it moves and has its being.

And when this influence, this growing self becomes such, or so self-centered, as to lose sight of that desire, purpose, aim to be *to* the glory of its source, and seeks rather FOR self, then it errs in its application of the influences within its abilities for the application of mind within its own experience.

Thus we find this entity capable of arousing others, or of becoming the incentive to and the motivative force of many—in and through its application of itself in the material world; as a worshipful experience to that something within the entity itself which magnifies—by the reflections—the awareness of the attributes of body, mind and soul in the experiences of others.

Hence the great intuitive forces, the abilities to raise the vibratory influence within the lives and the experiences of others through the use or the application of those abilities within their own selves—these become a part of the entity's experience; mentally first, and it grows either to that of materiality, material desire, or to those influences that are creative, constructive, spiritual in their nature.

Those things then as may be aroused by the self, by this entity, within the experiences of those it meets—either in close association or in casual meeting—may either create something that is material (which means only temporal), or something that is spiritual, that is eternal.

Then, as has been said: There is before thee this day life and death, good and evil. These are the ever present warring influences within materiality.

What then, ye ask, is this entity to do about, to do with, this ability of its own spiritual or psychic development; that may be made creative or may bring creative or destructive forces within the experiences of others?

"My Spirit beareth witness with thy spirit as to whether ye be the children of God or not." This becomes, then, that force, that influence for comparisons; as the entity meditates upon its own emotions, its own influences, these become very apparent within itself for comparisons.

Do they bespeak of kindness, gentleness, patience—that threshold upon which godliness appears?

Desire may be godly or ungodly, dependent upon the purpose, the aim, the emotions aroused.

Does it bring, then, self-abstinence? or does it bring self-desire?

Does it bring love? Does it bring long-suffering? Is it gentle? Is it kind?

Then, these be the judgments upon which the entity uses those influences upon the lives of others.

Does it relieve suffering, as the abilities of the entity grow? Does it relieve the mental anguish, the mental disturbances which arise? Does it bring also healing—of body, of mind, to the individual? Is it healed for constructive force, or for that as will bring pain, sorrow, hate and fear into the experience of others?

These be the judgments upon which the entity makes its choices, as it guides, directs or gives counsel to those who are seeking—seeking—What? That Light—which has become, which is, which ever was the light of the world!

What was that light? The Spirit of God moved, and there WAS light! That Light came—the light of men—yea, dwelt among men as *Mind* with the ability to choose, the ability to abstain, the ability to put away desire, hate, fear, and to put on the whole armor. All of these are attributes then of those influences and forces which are a part of the entity's experience.

And as these are applied, so may the entity come to apply its psychic abilities, its love, its desire, its hopes, *spiritualized* in self-effacement by placing God's *glory*, God's *love*, in the place of self; bringing hope, *hope* and *faith* in the minds and hearts, the lives of others.

This is the mission of the entity in this experience; fulfilling much of that sought after, much of that at times lost in self-desire. But often seeking, knowing, applying, ye become closer and closer in an at-onement with Him.

These are the purposes, these are the desires, these are the manners in which the mental may be applied for the soul and spiritual development; and in the manner, "As ye do it to the least of these, thy brethren, ye do it unto me," saith the Lord.

Ready for questions.

Q-1. Please give detailed directions for the entity regarding her mental and spiritual development through meditation. Outline the steps she should take that best fit her development.

A-1. First—as was indicated to these of old—purge or purify thy body—whether this be by mental means or by ablutions, do it in that manner as to satisfy thine own conscience.

Then, enter into the holy of holies of thine own inner self; for there He hath promised to meet thee. Let thy prayer be as this:

"As I surround myself with the consciousness of the Christ-Mind, may I—in body, in purpose, in desire—be purified to become the channel through which He may *direct* me in that *He*, the Christ, would have me do"; as respecting an individual, a condition, an experience. And as ye wait on Him, the answer will come.

Then each day *live*, towards those ye meet, in the same manner as ye prayed.

Q-2. Through what method or manner should my psychic abilities be expressed?

A-2. These, as we have just indicated, will be different with varied or different individuals.

Did He teach those at the well the same as those in the mount, or by the sea? Rather as He was given utterance, so gave He to others.

As has been indicated, the entity will find there are intuitive forces aroused by these applications of these purposes and desires. To some it will be healing, cooling the brow of those who are ill. To others it will be counseling as to this or that which disturbs their mental association, their moral lives, their material concepts. To others it will be as directing them to bear *their* cross even as He. For in Him does the burden become light, and the cross easy.

Q-3. Would it be possible for my psychic impressions to come through picture flashes?

A-3. These may come in varied forms. Possible; but know, as has been indicated, the tempter is ever about. That influence stands. Study well that which has been indicated here, and as ye apply it ye will know as to whether these influences of flashes, influences of writing, influences of speaking, arise from creative forces or dead selves.

Q-4. How may I recognize correct urges or hunches for action?

A-4. As just indicated; the manner being as has been directed, as to their sources and purposes. Not merely the flower. For remember, as indicated, many poisonous vines bear beautiful flowers. But what manner of seed? In what way are they constructive? Do they give a supply?

Think on these. There are few even of the foods for the body that are not of the seed of that sown for fruition.

Q-5. May I develop the power to heal others?

A-5. As indicated, this will *oft* be a part of thy experience. For, as indicated, the entity has the ability *innately!* As to how it manifests same, this becomes the job of the entity. To *create* in the minds of those it meets a desire for a worshipfulness toward the entity! What are the fruits, what are to be the fruits of these?

These depend upon what the entity does with that mind seeking—ever seeking light. Give the light—whether it is by song, by vision, by instruction, by healing.

Q-6. How may I develop psychic power for warnings of danger, difficulties to be avoided and opportunities to be taken advantage of, for myself, my children and others?

A-6. Let these be rather the outgrowth of the spiritual desire, rather than beginning with material manifestations, see?

For, these *are*—to be sure—a part of the whole, but if they are sought for only the material sustenance, material warning, material satisfaction, they soon become dead in their ability to be creative.   1947-3

See also:
Dreams in the Life of Prayer, Harmon H. Bro, Ph.D.

Chapter VII

USING PSYCHIC ABILITY

You can be your own psychic! Preceding chapters devoted to questions most often asked of psychics illustrate safe ways to get the answers yourself. The information in the readings reiterates many times the need for setting and living up to the highest ideal, the need for purifying oneself of all selfish and material desire.

Questions about various kinds of psychic phenomena were put to Edgar Cayce.

Q-2. How many kinds of psychic phenomena are known to mankind at the present time?
A-2. Almost as many as there are individuals, each entity being a force, or world within itself. Those of the unseen forces become then the knowledge of the individual, the power of expression, or of giving the knowledge obtained, being of an individual matter. 3744-1

One couple was given a technique for developing conscious telepathy.

Q-6. Give these entities the principle and technique of conscious telepathy.
A-6. The consciousness of His abiding presence. For, He is all power, all thought, the answer to every question. For, as these attune more and more to the awareness of His presence, the desire to know of those influences that may be revealed causes the awareness to become materially practical.

First, begin between selves. Set a definite time, and each at that moment put down what the other is doing. Do this for twenty days. And ye will find ye have the key to telepathy. 2533-7

If one were to conduct such an experiment, it would be well to examine the purpose for it.

Are the purposes, are the desires for the expression through the psychic influences or forces, of self? or have there been such experiences that other influences are seeking for expression?

This should first be determined, then, within not only the physical consciousness but the deeper consciousness of the entity.

Again this question should be answered within self: What is conscious service to the fellow men? Impelling them to think as self thinks? Or is it to enable such to find their *own* expression with their conscious contact with psychic forces?

Then again, what is meant, implied, by psychic development or a psychic experience of an entity?

Hence we see, in the question as is proposed, there is precluded in the consciousness of the entity that in which it believes as a manifestation or demonstration of psychic influences. Also, has the entity determined, and satisfied its mental and spiritual consciousness, as to *whom* the entity believes?

For as has been attested and demonstrated as of old, not every spirit, not every entity seeks to serve irrespective of self. Neither do all that may manifest seek to express or manifest other than that which has been the conscious, superconscious or subconscious desire of the ego.

What is thy purpose?

As we find, in defining then for the entity those questions, there must first be the purport—there must be the answer only within self—as to whom ye will serve. Is it God or man? Is it self or fame or fortune? Are there those grounds for common meeting of these influences?

For as the Teacher of teachers gave, as all who have pointed to a service to their fellow men, there is *one* God; or "The Lord thy God is *one*"—and the expression should be, "My Spirit (not spirits, but *my* spirit) beareth witness with *thy* spirit (not spirits) as to whether ye be the child of God or not."

That witness, that attesting, that direction then, is only—*only*—truly—in the temple of self. Or, as has been given of old, "Who shall I say has sent me? I AM THAT I AM!" That I AM then within self, responding to the I AM THAT I AM, is indeed the psychic or soul or of the soul self.

To arouse such then to an active service is to manifest the fruits of that spirit in conscious activity in a material world.

What then are these fruits? For the spirit itself may not be seen; for God hath not at any time been seen by man, only the manifested fruits of the spirit. Hence no hate, no dishonor; but patience, long-suffering, brotherly love, kindness, gentleness; not exalting of self but rather abasement of self that there may be the closer union, the closer walk with that I AM THAT I AM.

These be then those activities in which each soul may engage in a conscious material world. Not saying nor acting unkind things. No harsh words. None

of these are a part of the soul, that seeks for soul or psychic development.
These be the manners then that one may develop one's self.

This entity . . . has the abilities through the manifested activities in the earth for becoming an acoustic vessel for the expression of influences in a high vibratory force that brings into the experience a desire that is at times fearful, at times glorious, at times—well, shaking—in the wonderment of whether there may not be a losing of self in the very activities that go about self.

Hence all the more necessity for the entity to determine, and satisfy self's own consciousness, as to the question, "For what purpose would I enter into active, conscious service for my fellow men?" Is it that self may be exalted? Is it that self may be abased, that there may be the glory of God manifested among the children of men? or that an entity, a soul—as self—seeks expression that it, too, may use material consciousnesses for self-expression, self-glory? What witness does such an entity bear? That the Christ has come in the flesh, or that He beareth witness with thee in the deeds done in the body that are the fruits of the spirit of truth? or is it the indulgences into that which satisfies a longing for self-glory?

These questions must be answered, and may be answered in this:

Study to show thyself approved unto God, a workman not ashamed, rightly dividing the words of truth; and keeping self in body, in mind, unspotted from the world.

These be the determining factors, then, as to what, as to how, as to when, as to what way [1376] may develop her psychic abilities.

Ready for questions.

Q-1. Which of the following methods, if any, would be best for freeing this entity? Violet light, scopalamine (drug), hypnotism.

A-1. Neither of these. These have their place, in the *physical* forces of the body. Do not confuse that which is of spirit, and soul, and that which is of physical-mental and that is of the material. Put proper evaluations upon all phases.

For as the Triune is in the Father, the Son and the Holy Spirit, so is it in thy soul, thy mind, thy body. These are three, as the Triune are three, yet all in one.

What is the best manner? Enter into the holy of holies with thy God, for in the body are the manifestations of the Father, the Son, the Holy Spirit. Meditate, pray, read the Scriptures—these particularly:

The 30th of Deuteronomy, the first seven verses of the 6th of Joshua, the 23rd Psalm, the 1st Psalm, the 24th Psalm, the 150th Psalm; and know John 14, 15, 16, 17, not merely by heart—as rote—but as the *spirit* of the law, the love, the grace, the mercy, the truth that is expressed there. For as He hath given, "The earth, the heavens will pass away, but my words shall *not* pass away."

Know that the soul, the psychic forces of an entity, any entity, any body, are as eternal as that promise—for they are without days, without years, without numbers, but the *will* of man may make all at naught. For how *can* he be free unless will is a part of that Whole?

Thus, making the will one with Him, to be directed and guided by Him, you shall know the truth and the truth shall make you *free—you—*You—YOU!   1376-1

Only by making our wills one with His can we be free. This lady had asked about the use of light, drugs, and hypnotism and had been told not to confuse physical forces with spirit forces. What of automatic writing, Ouija boards and the like? The readings were consistent in advising people to stay away from them. Hugh Lynn Cayce's book, *Venture Inward,* in a chapter, "Dangerous Doorways to the Unconscious," describes in detail first-hand experience with people who had experimented with these lethal methods. Any method that involves a person's relinquishing his free will is not only detrimental to soul growth, but also to mental balance. God-given free will is the birthright of the soul, developed in daily choices. Giving up that will to another is tantamount to squandering the greatest inheritance.

But begin to study all phases of psychic phenomena, though don't begin with automatic writing. For this would soon lead to such channels as to be more detrimental than beneficial. But begin to read the Scripture, searching for those portions of same that give the warning, as well as the instruction as to how one would seek to be an individual who may give a great deal to mankind. This undertaken, the entity may set itself to be of a great help to others through any phase of psychic forces it would choose to demonstrate.

Know that it is not too far afield, but do gain thy understanding from beginning with this: Take Exodus 19:5. To be sure, it is interpreted by many here that the Creative Forces or God are speaking to a peculiar people. You were one of them. Why not, then, today? Although through the years your name has been changed, the soul is the same. Hence this is, as it were, spoken to thee.

Then take the 30th of Deuteronomy, where there is the admonition as to the source, that it's not from somewhere else, but it is within thine own self. For that influence of the Creative Force is so near, yea closer even than thy own hand!

Then analyze that, reading in connection with same all of the story of Ruth as to her sincerity. And if it needs to be, those companionships may be drawn from thine own activities, and the fear of what may be in the future will fade as the mists before the morning sun.

For in the study of these, not merely read to know them, but get the meaning of universal love, not attempting to make it personal but universal.

For God is love and, as ye go about to manifest same in thy conversation, ye may find the true meaning of love.

Study also astrological subjects, not as termed by some, but rather in the light of that which may be gained through a study of His word. For, as it was given from the beginning, those planets, the stars, are given for signs, for seasons, for years, that man may indeed (in his contemplation of the universe) find his closer relationships.

For man is made a co-creator with the Godhead. Not that man is good or bad according to the position of the stars, but the position of the stars brings what an individual entity has done about God's plan into the earth activities during those individual periods when man has the opportunity to enter or come into material manifestations.

In the study, forsake not, of course, the true way and light. As is given from the beginning: God said, "Let there be light" and there was light, and that light became, and is the light of the world. For it is true that light, that knowledge, the understanding of that Jesus who became the Christ, is indeed thy elder brother and yet Creator, Maker of the universe; and thus are ye a part of same and a directing influence.

Then, as ye practice His principles ye become aware of same. And these are first: "Thou shalt love the Lord thy God with all thy heart, thy mind, thy soul, and thy neighbor as thyself."   5124-1

Q-2. To further my work in possible radio reception of cosmic messages, should I attempt to train myself in automatic handwriting, or use a medium?

A-2. As has been indicated, rather than *automatic* writing *or* a medium, turn to the voice within! If this then finds expression in that which may be given to the self in hand, by writing, it is well; but not that the hand be guided by an influence outside of itself. For the universe, God, is within. Thou art His. Thy communion with the cosmic forces of nature, thy communion with thy Creator, is thy birthright! Be satisfied with nothing less than walking with Him!   1297-1

This excerpt shows a distinction the readings made between what was called "inspirational" writing and that known as "automatic writing." It indicates that one can follow one's own inner guidance, but should not surrender to an influence from without.

Q-8. Are the inspirational writings I receive to be relied upon as coming from a worthy and high source or should I not cultivate this form of guidance and information?

A-8. We would *not* from here counsel *anyone* to be guided by influences from without. For the *kingdom* is from within!

If these come as inspirational writings from within, and not as guidance from others—that is different!   1602-1

The lady [1376], whose reading appears earlier in the chapter, showed in the questions she asked a certain reliance on spirit guides. She was warned about letting her will be broken, and told how to protect herself.

Q-2. In what specific direction should she direct her activities for the greater possible benefit to mankind?

A-2. Healing!

Q-3. Are the methods recommended by her controls the proper ones for securing financial support which is needed?

A-3. "There is today set before thee good and evil, life and death—Choose thou!"

As we find, to be controlled or directed by an *entity* that has not *proclaimed*—Well, it is allowing will to be broken.

Do today the things thy hands, thy mind, thy body, find to do. Put thyself either in the hands of the I AM THAT I AM—or of the I AM that would seek first for self to be eased, or for self to be freed—or the earthly things and not the heavenly, the Godly.

Q-4. Are the entities who present themselves as guides for [1376] the persons they represent themselves to be and how far may their suggestions be followed for her best development?

A-4. Such questions are answered when those purposes, those desires have been determined within the inmost self of [1376].

How spoke he when he wrestled with the evil one regarding the physical body of Moses? Read that portion of Jude in which this is given.

Be ye not as the winds that blow about, as clouds without water; but be ye steadfast in the word of truth.

Q-5. How can Mr. [165] be of the greatest help to [1376]?

A-5. The greatest help would be to let her develop herself. Then aid in assisting and in applying a channel through which the abilities may reach material manifestations . . .

Q-8. Please explain how she may protect herself from these entities?

A-8. As an entity, a soul, a mind, enters—as has been so oft given—put about the self the cloak, the garment, yea the mantle of *Christ;* not as a man, not as an individual but the Christ—that universal consciousness of love that we see manifested in those who have forgotten self but—*as* Jesus—give themselves that others may know the truth.

For the promise has been, "If ye will call, I will *hear!*" "If ye will call, I *will hear!*"

That is the protection. Call—that the spirit of truth, that is manifested in the promises of an *All*-Loving Father, be about self in the seeking to aid, to bring cheer, hope, help, faith, courage to the weak, to the discouraged, to the disconsolate. These be the promises—and how hath it been said? "Though the heavens and the earth pass away, my words, my promises shall *not*"—unless ye supersede them by the promises of man! 1376-1

In a reading for a young electrical engineering student it was inferred that soul faculties and psychic forces are synonymous. Development of such forces, then, was equated with self-development. He was told not to be satisfied with any guide other than from the Throne of Grace itself. As he gets information by turning within, he is to question its source and meditate on its content. Above all, he is enjoined to keep self out of the way.

In giving that which may be the better or the correct manner of developing the soul faculties, or the psychic forces of the entity, this may be given better in the way and manner as a diet might be outlined for a physical body.

That from experience to experience there are found those things that do not answer at the time for the better expression or manifesting of the psychic and soul forces of a body, is the experience of each soul as it presses onward to the mark of the higher calling that is set in the ideal chosen by an entity to be guided by, or to parallel self's development with, or self's development towards.

But, as understood—or should be by each soul, the development must be *self*-development, *soul* development.

That the psychic faculties of a soul or entity are the manners through which manifestations may come from the outside and from within, is the experience of most individuals in their development; though they may call such manifestations by many names, that are seen or given under various lines of thought or various manners of development. Yet these expressions or manifestations are, as we would give, of the soul or the psychic faculties of the soul, or soul or spirit world.

Then, in the preparation for this entity, [440], as given, the body, the mind, the soul, is well balanced for a development. There are those experiences in the development that would tend to make for either very high development or for the turning of the development into destructive forces; not intentionally at all times, but that *tendency* for extravagance of self, as it were, in that direction. This, then, is rather as the warning:

First, as indicated, *find self*. Find what is self's ideal. And as to how high that ideal is. Does it consist of or pertain to materiality, or spirituality? Does it bespeak of self-development or selfless development for the glory of the ideal? And be sure that the ideal is rather of the spiritual. And this may become, as given, the first psychic experience of self's own inner soul, or self's own guide—as may be chosen. And do not be satisfied with a guide other than from the Throne of Grace itself! And when the self is being taught, seek a teacher. When self needs exhortation, then seek an exhorter. When self is desiring or seeking those channels that pertain to the material, or the application of material things, that spiritual lessons or spiritual truths may be brought, then *seek* such a source, such a channel for the *Creative* influences. And who better may be such a guide than the Creator *of* the universe? For, He has given that "If ye will seek me ye may find me" and "I will not leave thee comfortless" but if ye are righteous in purpose, in intent, in desire, "I will bring *all things* to thine remembrance" that are needs be for thy soul, thine mind, thine body, development.

This is a promise from Him, who is able to fulfill that which has been promised to every soul that seeks His face, His ways.

Then, speak oft with thy Maker. And let thine meditation be:

LORD, USE THOU ME IN THAT WAY, IN THAT MANNER, THAT I—AS THY SON, THY SERVANT—MAY BE OF THE GREATER SERVICE TO MY FELLOW MAN. AND MAY I KNOW HIS BIDDINGS, FATHER, AS THOU HAST PROMISED THAT IF WE WOULD HEAR HIM THAT WE ASK IN HIS NAME MAY BE OURS. I *CLAIM* THAT RELATIONSHIP, FATHER, AND I SEEK THY GUIDANCE DAY BY DAY!

And, as the light comes, as the feelings of the understandings come—never by chance, but in His ways doth He bring to pass that way, that channel, those individuals *through* whom self may make for *soul's* development—through those things that may come to thee, do ye walk in the Way.

This, then, is the manner for self to develop, for self to know, for self to understand.

Naturally, the question arises within self, how shall I know? In what manner will it be given me to know who is giving the information, who is speaking?

As outlined, first the answer is within self's own mental self, as to whatever is being sought.

Then in the meditation of that given in outline as a diet for the soul body, for the psychic faculties, the answer will be in the spirit. And each time, each experience when there is being sought for self as to what manner of activity or what manner or course is the right way to pursue, may it be given thee in the same way and manner.

If the approach is through some associate, some friend, some brother that is acting in the capacity as a sign, as a guide post along the way of life, then know that thou hast been guided to that way—and ye yourself must walk that road; and that ye may not walk alone—rather with His guiding hand will the way be shown, will the way be made plain in thine endeavors.

Keep self out of the way. Stumble not over the pitfalls that arise from self's anxiety, self's indulgences or self's expression of aggrandized interests—but let thy ways be His ways. Then ye shall know the truth and the truth shall make you free. 440-8

The next selection from a reading which gave advice on developing psychic abilities affirms that "the true God-forces meet within, not without, self" and that true psychic force is a manifestation of the Spirit. This manifestation can never be for self-aggrandizement. It must be the result of applying the divine law in one's own life and the spirits must be tested by their fruits.

Then, in the study of self there is the recognition that there are forces outside of self, there are forces and influences within self. The true God-forces meet within, not without self. For when there are altars builded outside, which individuals approach for the interpretation of law, whether it be physical, mental or spiritual, these are temptations. It is concerning such that warnings were given to the peoples. Though the entity or others may say, "Oh, that's the old Jewish conception of it," but be ye Jew, Gentile, Greek, Parthenian or what, the law is one—as God is one. And the first command is "Thou shalt have no other gods before me."

Then those influences without—know of whom they give evidence. It is true that ye have been warned, "Try ye the spirits." But this is also that that is questioned.

Rather then as we would give, so live in thine own life, in thine own application of the divine law, that there may be no question within self. And if ye live with the divine law, who may question? To be sure, there may be questions by some who have interpreted the law to their own understanding or their own undoing. Yet there is ever the answer "My Spirit beareth witness with thy spirit as to whether ye be the child of God or not."

These, then, should ever be. But there is produced by same humbleness—not as has been in some instances in the entity's self—not the lording of others. For as He gave, who was, who is, who ever will be the manifestation of the Spirit—which is true psychic force—he that will be the greatest will be the servant of all. Not necessarily being as a doormat, but ever willing, ever helpful—but to the glory of God, to the honor of self. Not to the glory of self in any manner or way, but in humbleness preferring one another.

These are the laws.   3548-1

This excerpt restates the fact that psychic information can be judged by its constructive application. It stresses the point that if such information is only for gratifying the carnal forces or that it emphasizes selfish motives, then it is not born of truth. It uses some interesting phraseology: "If it is only psychic, and of the earth earthy, then beware!" This indicates the necessity for testing impressions and information, for some influences can be from the material world.

Psychic is of the soul. As to whether psychic information is from those who have attuned themselves to the influences that are even in the material world, or to that force or source which has been sent or given in Creative Forces that are constructive in the experience of others, may only be judged by the application of same in the experience of the individual.

For, it has been given, "Search ye the Scriptures, for in them ye think ye have eternal life; and *they* be those that testify of me."

In this we see given that the soul which attunes itself through the manner of approach it, the soul, may make to the Creator of all life, all manifestations of life (which is that we worship as God), finds in the activity of individuals that which brings into the consciousness of others *that* individual's conception of that the individual worships.

If this makes for those conditions in the experience that are only the gratifying of the carnal forces, or to the aggrandizement of selfish motives, we then may know that it is not born of truth—but rather that which may be led from the path of light into those things that may seem right unto a man, yet the end thereof is death.

Then, how may one determine in one's own experience as to the value or the reliability of information that may be given through any channel that may propose to be, or that may be said to be, of a psychic nature—or with the divine illumination to the self? If it is only psychic and of the earth earthy, then beware! If it bespeaks of that which may bring *life* in its essence, or the spirit of truth that makes men free from those things that hinder them from knowing more of the truth, of the *spirit* of truth in the earth, then it may bring that which is constructive into the experience of those that receive same.

"Try ye the spirits," ye have been admonished; and they that testify that He has *come*, that bespeak such in their activities, are of *truth*.

Then, they that bring to each soul—not comfort, not as earthly pleasure, but—that which is *spiritually constructive in the experience of a soul, are worthy of acceptation.*   5752-5

The readings state that psychic development is soul development, and they are consistent in their suggestions for this. They are also consistent in stating that information thus received is for the soul's own help and not to guide or control others.

Here we have an emotional body well versed in the study of meditation, the study of transmission of thought, with the ability to control others.

Don't control others. Suppose thy God controlled thee without thy will? What would you become, or what would you have been?

But you were made in the image of thy Creator, to be a companion with Him—not over someone else, but a companion with thy brother and not over thy brother. Hence do not act that way, because ye have the greater ability or greater knowledge of control of others . . .

The abilities are unlimited, but as the warnings are given in Exodus as well as in Deuteronomy, know how they may be centralized for thy brethren in "The Lord is my shepherd" and not Mr. [3428] but thy Lord, thy God.

3428-1

80

You can be *your own psychic,* but nowhere is it suggested that you should be someone else's psychic! This ability should not be misused, that is, used for selfish, ego-building purposes, nor should it be used to control others. The best and only way to guide is by the example of living according to divine law.

Q-7. Are there any general directions you can give me for the helping or guidance of my family or friends?

A-7. As ye study to show thyself approved, as the entity itself is acceptable—not only by precept but example—these become manners and ways in which there may be counsel in all that *is* done, if these are kept.

1602-1

Q-15. What is meant by "may this *entity, applying same with the life as led by the Master, guide many," and how may the entity best proceed to do this?*

A-15. *Live* it! *LIVE* it! Not as a tenet, not as a theory, not as a hope. *Live* it! even as the Master lived it.

256-2

Across the world many troubled people seek out a variety of psychics and would-be psychics for help and positive reinforcement. The Edgar Cayce readings assure us that we can all develop psychic ability, and that the safest and truest way to get the answers we need is to turn within. Over and over they assure us that His promises are true today and forever.

The greater research is this:

Remember the promise He has given, "If ye abide with me, I will bring to thy remembrance *all things from the foundation of the world!*" What a vision—that ye yourself, through that promise, that power, may know; not only how ye have acted towards others but may gain a glimpse . . . of *thy* vibration, and as to how ye have affected others.

1581-2

Q-1. What is the highest possible psychic realization . . . ?

A-1. That God, the Father, speaks directly to the sons of men—even as He has promised.

440-4

THE EDGAR CAYCE LEGACIES

Among the vast resources which have grown out of the late Edgar Cayce's work are:

The Readings: Available for examination and study at the Association for Research and Enlightenment, Inc.,(A.R.E.®) at Virginia Beach, Va., are 14,256 readings consisting of 49,135 pages of verbatim psychic material plus related correspondence. The readings are the clairvoyant discourses given by Cayce while he was in a self-induced hypnotic sleep-state. These discourses were recorded in shorthand and then typed. Copious indexing and cross-indexing make the readings readily accessible for study.

Research and Information: Medical information which flowed through Cayce is being researched and applied by the research divisions of the Edgar Cayce Foundation. Work is also being done with dreams and other aspects of ESP. Much information is disseminated through the A.R.E. Press publications, *A.R.E. News* and *The A.R.E. Journal.* Coordination of a nationwide program of lectures and conferences is in the hands of the Department of Education. A library specializing in psychic literature is available to the public with books on loan to members. An extensive tape library has A.R.E. lectures available for purchase. Resource material has been made available for authors, resulting in the publication of scores of books, booklets and other material.

A.R.E. Study Groups: The Edgar Cayce material is most valuable when worked with in an A.R.E. Study Group, the text for which is *A Search for God,* Books I and II. These books are the outcome of eleven years of work by Edgar Cayce with the first A.R.E. group and represent the distillation of wisdom which flowed through him in the trance condition. Hundreds of A.R.E. groups flourish throughout the United States and other countries. Their primary purpose is to assist the members to know their relationship to their Creator and to become channels of love and service to others. The groups are nondenominational and avoid ritual and dogma. There are no dues or fees required to join a group although contributions may be accepted.

Membership: A.R.E. has an open-membership policy which offers attractive benefits.

For more information write A.R.E., Box 595, Virginia Beach, Va. 23451. To obtain information about publications, please direct your query to A.R.E. Press. To obtain information about joining or perhaps starting an A.R.E. Study Group, please direct your letter to the Study Group Department.